T0282742

BRUCE SPRINGSTEEN

BRUCE SPRINGSTEEN

AN ILLUSTRATED BIOGRAPHY

MEREDITH OCHS

chartwell
books

CONTENTS

INTRODUCTION

Few artists are omnipresent in popular culture for any sustained period. Fewer still are known to the public on a first-name basis. Although you're as likely to hear the name Springsteen by itself, say "Bruce" and almost any music fan will know exactly who you're talking about.

Since releasing his first album, *Greetings from Asbury Park, N.J.*, in 1973, Bruce Springsteen has become a peerless rock star. A ferociously prolific songwriter, a tireless performer, a musician who forged enduring ties that bind with bandmates (the E Street Band) and a record label he has called home for more than four decades (Sony/Columbia), an artist with the rare ability to court controversy without losing a lot of fans, he's an anomaly in the music business.

And Bruce is ubiquitous, much like Elvis Presley, the first rock 'n' roller he idolized, except that Springsteen is alive and very active. His eighteenth studio album, 2014's *High Hopes*, marked his eleventh number 1 record in the United States. Only the Beatles and Jay Z have had more number 1 records stateside than Bruce. It's nearly impossible to

---

go a day without hearing one of his songs on the radio, or in a supermarket, or at a dining spot. He tours the world relentlessly, sometimes logging around a hundred shows a year. That statement doesn't do justice to Springsteen's live show, a maelstrom of rock energy clocking in at three-plus hours, continually invigorated by improvisation, fan interaction, and freshly worked-up covers as varied as Mack Rice's "Mustang Sally" and Van Halen's "Jump." (His band added horn arrangements to the latter and trotted it out for the first time ever to open his Dallas, Texas, show on April 6, 2014.) Like Elvis and another son of New Jersey, Frank Sinatra, he has his own twenty-four-hour channel, E Street Radio, on Sirius XM. He turns up in literature, not only in books about him but also inspired by him, from Stephen King's *The Stand*, to T. C. Boyle's collection *Greasy Lake & Other Stories*, to *Meeting Across the River*, an anthology triggered by his song of the same name.

Springsteen also appears in many movies and TV shows. His voice is the first one you hear in the remarkable Oscar-winning 2013 documentary on backup singers, *20 Feet from Stardom*. Cinematic to begin with, Bruce's songs have long been used to great effect in film soundtracks—he won an Oscar for the song he wrote for the highly acclaimed and awarded *Philadelphia*, he was nominated for

his contribution to *Dead Man Walking*, and he nabbed a Golden Globe for his song in *The Wrestler*. More recently, he was heard in *Warm Bodies*, a zombie romantic comedy (yes, there is such a thing as a zom-rom-com), and the dark drama *The Place Beyond the Pines*. He also did a brilliant cameo in Stephen Frears's film adaptation of Nick Hornby's *High Fidelity*, and was the subject of the in-depth Ridley Scott–produced film, *Springsteen & I*, that explores the unique relationship between Bruce and his fans.

His songs have turned up on scripted prime-time television, including the series finale of *Sons of Anarchy*, *Glee*, *The Good Wife*, and *The Office*. He has appeared with Jimmy Fallon on *Late Night* and *The Tonight Show* for several hilarious song parodies, disguised as younger versions of himself. Those clips, viewed millions of times on YouTube, confirm that despite his sincerity and the gravitas of his work, he is a deeply funny man who doesn't appear to take himself too seriously.

Springsteen's lyrics are vernacular, melded with vivid character sketches, biblical metaphors, heartland imagery, and social consciousness. So expansive is his cultural context that you can study him at major American universities, even the Ivy League. Princeton has offered a course, Sociology from E Street, that explores "Bruce Springsteen's America." The University of Rochester once gave a history class devoted to his work. At Rutgers, you could study theology through the prism of his lyrics, which may make the most sense to those fans who describe his concerts as a religious experience. You could also pray on him at the Trinity Episcopal Cathedral in Portland, Oregon, which held a "Bruce Springsteen Eucharist." And in July 2014, he earned even greater pop culture status when he received his own category on the television game show *Jeopardy!*

His fans are not the only ones who love him. The camera loves Springsteen, as much now at age seventy-plus as ever. He looks like the rock star the world expects, with a brooding, craggy face that always seems to catch the right light, tousled hair, and an intense expression that only hints at his preternatural work ethic. Again, like his idol Elvis, he has had distinct, instantly identifiable "eras," minus the hefty, white-jumpsuited Vegas years, of course—a self-proclaimed fitness devotee, Bruce has stayed in remarkable shape throughout his life. But whether captured in a white tank top and tan during his early Jersey Shore years, bedraggled with his big boho hat or decked out in a suit jacket in the mid-1970s, the red bandana head wrap or bolo tie of the 1980s, or the dark shirts and vests he settled into later on, Springsteen has always been a compelling subject for photographers. As good as his portraiture is, he's even better to behold during his sweat-soaked,

ABOVE | Opening night of *The Rising* tour, August 7, 2002, on his home turf at the Continental Airlines Arena, NJ. Bruce got the audience to raise their hands with him during the song "Lonesome Day" from his album *The Rising*.

unpredictable performances, where he's likely to jump up on a piano and crowd-surf.

There's also the matter of New Jersey, where Springsteen was born, nurtured, and lives today. The state is maligned for its heavily tolled turnpike, blighted cities, and many refineries, along with the caricatures of its populace and their big hair, the tanning culture, and the liberal bending of vowels that punctuates the regional accent. Even though he is an American artist with a global fan base, in the United States his name is practically synonymous with this state, yet in a positive way. When New Jersey gets laughed at, it's likely to be followed by "Yeah but . . . what about Springsteen." Never mind that New Jersey is associated with Meryl Streep, Derek Jeter, Tom Cruise, Anne Hathaway, Shaquille O'Neal, Whitney Houston, Michael Douglas, Bon Jovi, Queen Latifah, Bruce Willis, Yogi Berra, Martha Stewart, not to mention countless other celebrities and the show *The Sopranos*. Springsteen is the one who gives the state its biggest lift. He fashioned Jersey into song, capturing its blue-collar families and its seaside towns with their carnivalesque revelry and gritty reality. He could make New Jersey romantic and its people noble. He distinguished himself from Americana rock artists by virtue of his environs. At the Pennsylvania border, there's a sign that claims it's "where America begins," but for Springsteen and his fans, New Jersey is and will always be where it begins.

ABOVE | Bruce and photographer Lynn Goldsmith were dating in 1978, the year she took this photo.

RIGHT | Bruce Springsteen, Patti Scialfa, and Steven Van Zandt singing at The Fleet Center in Boston on October 4, 2002. The finale included Peter Wolf of the J. Geils Band on a version of the Standells' "Dirty Water."

1

MY HOMETOWN

Just about thirty miles east of the Pennsylvania border sits the township of Freehold, New Jersey. Bruce Frederick Joseph Springsteen made his September 23, 1949 debut at Monmouth Memorial Hospital in nearby Long Branch and spent his formative years in Freehold. Its schools, churches, neighborhoods, and kids all went into shaping the artist he'd become. It's where the family relationships that defined the arc of his songwriting and ultimately of his career unfolded. It gave the world one of the biggest rock stars of all time, and the world is still taking him in.

It was in Freehold that Springsteen began to display glimpses of the innate gifts that he'd nurture into greatness. Small and shy, he developed a physicality and an utter commitment to music that proved to be early indicators of his exceptionalism.

Springsteen friend and cohort Richard Blackwell played conga on his second album *The Wild, the Innocent & the E Street Shuffle*. He grew up with Bruce and knew him from school and their Freehold neighborhood. Blackwell recalls Bruce as extraordinarily agile, not in a way that suggested supreme athleticism but one that would presage his signature stage moves. Back then, Blackwell, his brother, and friends passed their winter afternoons making snowballs, and, like bored suburban kids in cold climates everywhere, tossed them at people walking by and other moving objects.

He remembers one of the first times he saw Bruce. "We see this kid coming out of his house," Blackwell says. "My brother tried to pick him off, I tried to pick him off. Nobody could ever hit him. He knew how to move."

"Everybody knew him," he says. "He always had his guitar on his back. We knew he wasn't going play no baseball, wasn't going to be no football player." Friends remember him as being slight until around age twelve.

But Bruce did and still does love baseball—he played right fielder in Little League until the guitar won over bats and gloves. He was even inducted into the Little League Museum Hall of Excellence at Little League International, in South Williamsport, Pennsylvania, in 1997. He wasn't able to make a career out of baseball, but he did get one of his biggest hits, "Glory Days," out of his experience on the field, along with countless hours of onstage patter. In the song, he writes about a speedball pitcher based on his real-life teammate and friend Joe DePugh, who was a good enough player to be invited

to try out for the Los Angeles Dodgers in his senior year of high school (even though he didn't make the team). He was also a good enough friend to be able to tease Bruce about his baseball skills and bestow upon him the nickname Saddie.

DePugh says he and Springsteen have run into each other on occasion over the years, most recently at an Italian restaurant in Freehold around 2009. Before they both left, Bruce revealed to DePugh that his connections to the place where he grew up and its people were more than just career-making inspiration; they were a deep and abiding part of him.

"He said, 'Always remember, I love you,' not like some corny Budweiser commercial, but a real sentimental thing," DePugh says. "I was dumbfounded. I said, 'Thanks, Saddie.' That was all I could come up with, and all of a sudden, he's out the door. And it hit me that you've got to do a little better than that, so I pulled the door open and yelled down to him, 'Sad!' He turned around and I pointed at him and said, 'I love you, too, and I'm real proud of you.' And he just waved."

Bruce was the first child born to Douglas (Dutch, as he was sometimes called) and Adele Springsteen. Virginia came along the year after Bruce was born—named after Dutch's sister who was hit by a truck while riding her tricycle and killed at age

Bruce Springsteen

SCHOLARSHIP

EXPLANATION OF MARKS

Ex.	Excellent	F.	Fair
V.G.	Very Good	P.	Poor (Just Passing)
Av.	Average	B.	Below Grade Level

	I 30 da.	II 30 da.	III 30 da.	Exam.	IV 30 da.	V 30 da.	VI 30 da.	Exam.	Yearly Attainments
RELIGION					Av.	Av.	Av.		Av.
READING*					Av.	Av.	Av.		Av.
Understands when reading silently									
Reads orally with expression									
LANGUAGE*									
Takes part in oral composition									
Uses correct English									
Enjoys good poetry and good stories									
SPELLING†									
WRITING†					F.	F.	F.		F.
ARITHMETIC†					B.	P.	P.		P.

* Check principal powers (√)
† Not required in grade one

Recommendation at the end of the year:

Assigned to Grade 2   Date *June 15, 1956*

Teacher *Sr. Anne Mary*

EVIDENT QUALITIES

EXPLANATION OF MARKS

C—Commendable
S—Satisfactory (in all qualities unless otherwise noted)
U—Unsatisfactory

	I 30 da.	II 30 da.	III 30 da.	IV 30 da.	V 30 da.	VI 30 da.	Yearly Attainments
PERSONAL and SOCIAL				S	S	S	S
Punctuality							
Sociability							
Obedience							
Self-reliance							
Co-operation							
Self-control							
STUDY HABITS				S	S	S	S
Application							
Perseverance							
HEALTH HABITS				S	S	S	S
Obedience to ordinary rules							
ATTENDANCE Days Present				28	27	26	
Days Absent				2	2	1	
Times Tardy							

five. Virginia would later introduce Bruce to George Theiss of the Castiles (the first band Bruce recorded with), and her married life would inspire Bruce's song "The River." Bruce was thirteen when his parents had Pamela, who would grow up to be an actress and photographer. Adele made sure her son understood what was happening during the pregnancy. "She really took me through the whole thing," Bruce says. "We used to sit on the couch and watch TV, and she'd say, 'Feel this,' and I'd put my hand on her stomach and I'd feel my little sister in there. And from the very beginning, I had a deep connection with her."

The Springsteens were Roman Catholic, and for Bruce that meant mandatory church on Sunday, participation as an altar boy, and attending St. Rose of Lima Catholic School. Cleveland, Ohio's Rock and Roll Hall of Fame and Museum displays a photo of an eight-year-old Springsteen at his first communion. Catholicism gave him both a rich spiritual life and a deep trench from which he'd draw songwriting inspiration, something to guide his conscience, and something to rebel against. He famously explains why he realized early on that organized religion was not for him:

"In the third grade a nun stuffed me in a garbage can under her desk because, she said,

ABOVE | Bruce's first grade report card from the Diocese of Trenton, St. Rose of Lima Catholic School, Freehold, NJ, June 15, 1956. He may have preferred the guitar to academics, but he still advanced to the second grade.

that's where I belonged. I also had the distinction of being the only altar boy knocked down by a priest during Mass.

"I quit the stuff [religion] when I was in eighth grade. By the time you're older than thirteen it's too ludicrous to go along with anymore. By the time I was in eighth grade I just lost it all."

But Springsteen has repeatedly invoked the "once a Catholic, always a Catholic" axiom. Faith has manifested itself in his lyrics ever since his first audition for record producer John Hammond at Columbia in 1972. Springsteen played a few songs for Hammond that day, including ones that made it onto his first album ("The Angel" and "It's Hard to Be

a Saint in the City") and one that didn't—"If I Was the Priest." When Hammond heard the last one, he said, "Bruce, that's the damnedest song I've ever heard. Were you brought up by nuns?"

In fact, the theological virtues of religion—faith, hope, and charity—had a lasting impact not only on Springsteen but also on the way he connected with his audience. He bent biblical imagery and language and infused them into his songs and concerts, and as his conscience progressed over the years, he added a deep commitment to exploring social and economic issues. He put his fame and money behind causes and candidates who, in his opinion, stood for justice. He extracted the parts of faith most important to him, choosing humanity over doctrine.

As for hope, it first arrived when he was nine in the form of a guitar, rented for him by Adele. After seeing Elvis Presley on *the Ed Sullivan Show*, Springsteen told her that he wanted to be just like Elvis; he said he couldn't understand why anyone wouldn't want to be Elvis. When he failed to master the instrument quickly—as any kid does the first time they felt the bite of guitar strings in their soft, fleshy fingertips—he gave up, only to return to it at thirteen. His mother once again helped him acquire his first real guitar, and then his second one, the Kent that he'd play in teenage bands.

ABOVE | Childhood friends say Bruce was on the small side during his freshman year of high school, 1964.

He acknowledged her contribution in his acceptance speech for the Rock and Roll Hall of Fame: "I'd like to thank my mother, Adele," he said, "for that slushy Christmas Eve, that Christmas Eve—a night like the one outside—when we stood outside the music store, and I pointed at that sunburst guitar, and she had that sixty bucks, and I said, 'I need that one.' She got me what I needed, and she protected me, and provided for me a thousand other days and nights. As importantly, she gave me a sense of work as something that was joyous, and that filled you with pride and self-regard, and that committed you to your world."

Springsteen never put the instrument down again. It was his workhorse, the long-term project of mastering it launched in a fury during months of intense playing in his bedroom. He immersed himself in it and brought it everywhere. He wasn't playing the role of a loner who dragged a guitar around on his back; he really was one. In some ways, he still is. Friends remember him showing up at parties where there were girls, drinking, and drugs, only to ignore the revelry and disappear with his ax.

Photographs of Bruce as a student at Freehold Regional High School leave little impression other than perhaps of a shop class kid bound to follow in his dad's footsteps through a lifetime of odd jobs. His yearbook

photo shows an ordinary boy with a thick comb-over and teeth that appear uncorrected by proper orthodontia. Another, earlier photo shows a slight but smiling adolescent, full of energy, upright in his seat, ready to bound right off the page. Though he was innately smart and would eventually devour books by American authors that directly shaped his songs, academics were not his strong suit.

But music was, even though Springsteen's Kent "sounded awful," according to bandmate Jay Gibson, a member of the Rogues, the first band Bruce joined as a rhythm guitarist. Gibson says Bruce couldn't keep it in tune. "All I ever remember saying to him was that he'd really need to get a new guitar 'cause it wouldn't stay in tune."

Determined, Bruce practiced guitar until, in 1965, he was good enough to join

ABOVE | Bruce's 1967 high school senior yearbook has been listed on eBay for $2,499.

the Castiles, a teenage group managed by local music benefactor Tex Vinyard that performed in and around Freehold. His audition was so intense that afterward lead singer George Theiss apparently asked Vinyard, "Am I still the front man?" Bruce got up to speed quickly, learning lead guitar parts, some of them from bassist Frank Marziotti. Already in his twenties, Marziotti was recruited by Vinyard primarily because he owned a gas station where the band could practice, but he also served as both a good example of professionalism and as a tutor to the younger musicians. He remembers Bruce as a quick study. "I knew he was a brilliant boy. He was a fast learner and he was ambitious," he says. Before long, Springsteen became a "second" front man, trading vocal duties with George.

There was a rivalry, but "they worked it out between them," according to Marziotti.

With a bit of money put into the band by Tex Vinyard (it was a labor of love for him, according to Marziotti, and he bankrolled it himself), the Castiles garnered a local following, playing at swim clubs, Elks Lodges, and VFWs, and eventually Cafe Wha? in New York City. "Bruce and the Castiles were one of the better bands," says childhood friend Joseph Bacenko. "Bruce's music, just by himself, was good enough to go somewhere. They were very refined for a young group."

But the more he got into music, the greater the tension between Bruce and his father became. The arguments between the two would inform Springsteen's stage banter for years, another hallmark of his live show.

ABOVE | The Castiles, Bruce's first professional band, in a 1965 promotional photo. L to R: Frank Marziotti, Paul Popkin, George Theiss, Vinnie Manniello, and Springsteen.

"He asked me what I thought I was doing with myself," Bruce said between songs in 1976 at the Palladium in New York City. "And we'd always end up screaming at each other. My mother, she'd always end up running in from the front room crying, and trying to pull him off me, try to keep us from fighting with each other . . . I'd always end up running out the back door and pulling away from him. Pulling away from him, running down the driveway screaming at him, telling him, telling him, telling him how it was my life and I was going to do what I wanted to do."

The drama of the Springsteens' Freehold home is pervasive in songs such as "Adam Raised a Cain" and "Independence Day," disillusionment and gloom echoing through dark corridors, the ruminations of a child growing aware in an unenlightened household, a "TV house," as Springsteen once said, where there was "not a lot of book reading."

Much of the discontentment stemmed from Douglas Springsteen, who brought to his family a fair amount of sadness. His sister's death had cast an intractable, lasting pall over the family. Douglas dropped out of high school and enlisted in the army, serving in World War II when he was still a teenager. From many accounts, he struggled with bipolar disorder and was prone to depression and fits of rage, and among his three kids, he directed his ire most frequently at his only son. E Street Band guitarist and longtime Springsteen cohort Steven Van Zandt remembers Douglas Springsteen as being "scary," but he acknowledges that members of the "Greatest Generation" had no frame of reference to deal with their kids coming of age in the 1960s.

Douglas had a hard time staying employed in an era when employment was growing scarce. Freehold, like Trenton and many centers of industry, had enjoyed its own mid-twentieth-century heyday, with a cannery, an iron foundry, and a branch of the Sigmund Eisner shirt factory, which outfitted the Boy Scouts of America and provided uniforms to the U.S. government; it was immortalized in Bruce's song "My Hometown."

Freehold was also home to A. & M. Karagheusian's rug mill, where Douglas worked for a time, which loomed carpet

ABOVE | Bruce's first recording. Local Freehold music patron Tex Vineyard managed and funded the Castiles, including this original 45 test pressing of "Baby I," recorded on May 18, 1966 at Mr. Music Inc. in Bricktown, NJ, and later signed by Bruce ("Here's the first!").

for Radio City Music Hall in 1932 and the U.S. Supreme Court building in 1933. But in 1964, the year after cofounder Arshag Karagheusian died, the rug mill shut down for good, taking fifteen hundred jobs with it. As the 1960s progressed, racial tensions emerged in the economically challenged town. Fires consumed two big swaths of its main street. If the world felt like it was slipping away, that sense of uneasiness must have echoed deeper in Springsteen as he observed his dad being unable to provide for his family, leaving his mom to be the breadwinner, as he recalled onstage:

"My mom, she was a secretary, and she worked downtown . . . And my father, he worked a lot of different places. He worked in a rug mill for a while, he drove a cab for a while, and he was a guard down at the jail for a while. I can remember when he worked down there, he used to always come home real pissed off, drunk, sit in the kitchen. At night, nine o'clock, he used to shut off all the lights, every light in the house, and he used to get real pissed off if me or my sister turned any of them on. And he'd sit in the kitchen with a six-pack, a cigarette . . ."

Douglas's demons and Freehold's troubled times had a lifelong impact on Springsteen. From Bruce's determination to be his own boss and to live life on his own terms, to his own battles with clinical depression many years later, they informed his songwriting, the tales he would come to tell night after night onstage, and even the way he created a new "family" with the E Street Band.

ABOVE | Circa 1950s postcard picturing Bruce's hometown of Freehold, NJ, which experienced hard economic times in the 1960s that would have a profound effect on Springsteen's music.

RIGHT | New Year's Eve, December 31, 1977, at the Capitol Theatre in Passaic, NJ. Bruce and the E Street Band joined Southside Johnny and the Asbury Jukes onstage, then played their own set.

ESCAPE

So much of Springsteen's early work abounds with the desire to "escape." In postwar blue-collar neighborhoods, where families watched the burgeoning American dream from a distance but rarely could access it, there was a lot from which to escape: a hometown in decline, a futureless job, an emotionally fraught family, teenage frustration, the draft. Like Marlon Brando's Johnny Strabler in *The Wild One*, when asked what he was rebelling against, the gang leader replied, "Whaddya got?" The songs Bruce heard on his mom's kitchen radio, like the Animals' "We Gotta Get Out of This Place," only fanned the flames.

The first place to which Springsteen could actually escape was Asbury Park, a seaside community fifteen miles east of Freehold. Kids would bike there from surrounding suburban towns, Robert Blackwell says. Founded in the late 1800s as a resort town by the Atlantic Ocean, Asbury Park offered beach and boardwalk, but by the late 1960s, it had become an extraordinary scene for musicians.

At 702 Cookman Avenue, on a street that runs diagonally along the south side of

Asbury Park, sat a Thom McAn shoe store. Just above it, the rock 'n' roll sound of the Jersey Shore was incubating. One floor up was the Green Mermaid Café, and above that was a large room with a short wooden stage that stretched across the far end. It was the Upstage, an alcohol-free after-hours club where predawn jam sessions were held from 1968 through 1971. Both the café and club were run by Tom and Margaret Potter, husband-and-wife hairstylists who loved the arts and cultivated a bohemian lifestyle. Carrie Potter-Devening, Tom's granddaughter, says the prototype for the club began in the couple's apartment, right above their beauty shop and filled with Tom's artwork. The Potters would hold parties at their place for creative friends—photographers, poets, artists—entertaining in their rooftop garden. It was where they conceived the Upstage, a place where they could encourage musicians to get together, exchange ideas, and, above all, play original music, in contrast with much of Asbury Park's bar scene at the time.

Twenty years Tom's junior and his third wife, Margaret took up guitar and formed her own band, Margaret and the Distractions, which became the residing house band at the Green Mermaid. The café would close at night and then the Upstage would open until around five in the morning. The Potters had apparently built amplifiers into the wall,

so anyone could show up, borrow a guitar, and plug in and play. The club's décor, tinged with a psychedelic paint job, had a vibe more reminiscent of San Francisco hippiedom than a shore town. Devening says her grandfather had even made a sign for the club that said LEAVE YOUR ANGER AND HATE OUTSIDE WITH YOUR BOOZE AND DRUGS.

Ironically, it was around the time Bruce found his way to the Upstage that his parents moved to Northern California. Encouraged to head out west by Bruce's girlfriend at the time, the story goes that they quickly realized they didn't belong in a bastion of grooviness like San Francisco, and Adele Springsteen was directed to the more provincial San Mateo area after asking someone at a gas station, "Where do people like us live?"

Bruce stayed behind when his folks left the East Coast, and after convincing his local draft board that he was unfit for service, studying for a brief spell at Ocean County College, and ultimately getting evicted from his parents' old house, he moved to Asbury Park and found himself in the center of a musical maelstrom. "Bruce was in the right place at the right time and he knew it," says Frank Marziotti.

"We had a nice community of musicians in that area," says Albee Tellone, a friend and early roadie for Bruce. Tellone played a number of instruments and was immersed

in the Asbury Park scene, performing at the Upstage and sharing an apartment with Steve Van Zandt and "Southside Johnny" Lyon. "If you needed a bass player or a drummer, there was always someone." Tellone was playing acoustic sets at the Green Mermaid Café and remembers that "Bruce hung out at the Upstage all the time whenever he didn't have a gig." The Potters' no alcohol policy wasn't an issue as Bruce wasn't much of a drinker and never touched drugs. Fear of inheriting his father's psychological problems made him want to be in control of his mind. Van Zandt has said that Springsteen is "the only guy I know—I think the only guy I know at all—who never did drugs." It was unusual for the time.

Even in a town full of musicians, Springsteen distinguished himself. He "just had this enormous appetite to play," said musician and early bandmate Vinnie Roslin, who passed away in 2012. "He'd play anywhere, anytime for anybody. He was like a television set with one channel, and on that channel was 'practice music.'" He didn't look for a job—creating music would be his vocation. Bruce's dedication had only grown more complete from his days locked away in his

ABOVE | Steel Mill at the Green Mermaid, one floor below The Upstage in January 1971. L to R: Bruce, a female fan, Vini Lopez, Robbin Thompson, Steve Van Zandt, Danny Federici.

Freehold bedroom, where he'd been holed up with his guitar. Normal kinds of activities fell by the wayside, like finding a place to live—it was catch-as-catch-can for a while—or going to the DMV. According to Robbin Thompson, singer of the band Mercy Flight who played with Bruce in the band Steel Mill for a short time, Springsteen at twenty-one still hadn't bothered to get his driver's license—strange for a kid in highway-predominant New Jersey, and stranger still for a guy who would write so many songs about cars.

Most of Asbury Park's bars were rife with professional cover bands that catered to a Top 40–loving audience. "They had some great players over there [at the beach bars]," Tellone recalls. But when the bars shut down, the Upstage was just getting warmed up. The scene's "big guys would come over after their set and just jam," he says. "Bruce would get them to play, they'd play twenty-five-minute songs." The Upstage was where Springsteen's burgeoning skills as not only a singer and guitarist but also as a bandleader were on display, and people took notice. "He was animated, and he had a look about him, this intangible magnetism, and an honesty about what he did," Thompson says.

"Even then, as a young guy, he was already one of the best live performers I'd ever seen," says Carl "Tinker" West, Bruce's former manager. "He played guitar all right,

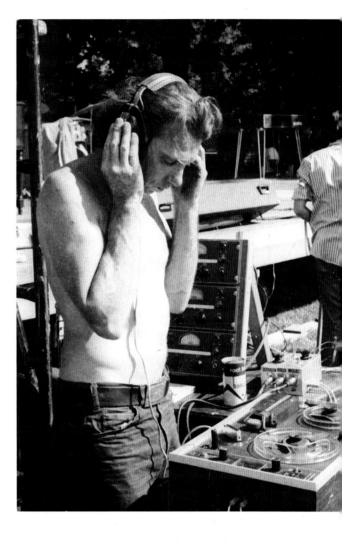

but he knew how to sing and he knew how to communicate with an audience. He put fire into it, and it worked." Tinker's equation for a successful performance didn't involve what he thought of the music, whether he liked it or not, or what anyone in particular thought; instead, he gauged the reaction of the crowd. If the crowd loved it, he knew he was on to something, and the crowd loved Bruce.

Tinker West is, to this day, a fascinating polymath: a musician, engineer, bona fide rocket scientist (he worked for NASA), and

LEFT | Bruce during his days in the band Child, playing a Labor Day 1969 show held at a section of East Long Branch nicknamed "Freak Beach" by locals.

ABOVE | Carl "Tinker" West recording the first known performance of the Bruce Springsteen Band at the "Second Annual Nothings Festival," held at Brookdale Community College in Lincroft, NJ, on July 10, 1971.

entrepreneur who also happened to be an extraordinary surfboard craftsman. He moved from California to the Jersey Shore in 1966 and opened Challenger East Surfboards in Wanamassa, just a mile and a half northwest of Asbury Park.

While living in the San Francisco area, Tinker had observed the growth of hippie culture and music, so it's no surprise that he gravitated toward the Upstage, with its swirling Day-Glo paint job and highly creative atmosphere. It was here that Tinker heard Bruce play and where Tom Potter introduced Tinker to Vini Lopez, a drummer who had seen Bruce play with a band called Earth. After a particularly sweaty Upstage jam with

Bruce, Lopez says he thought it might be a good idea to start a new band.

Lopez says Tinker had just made him an offer: put together a band that played original music and he would manage and promote it. That band would consist of Lopez, bassist Vinnie Roslin, keyboardist Danny Federici, and Bruce. They called themselves Child for a short time, then Steel Mill. They played phenomenally well together, so tightly that "you could hear the other guy breathe," Roslin said. With Tinker backing them, their aspirations were lofty.

Tinker had been around the music business in California and had a passion for it. He also had everything that Springsteen and his

ABOVE | Tinker West's Challenger East Surfboards Factory in Wanamassa, NJ, near Asbury Park, was also a rehearsal space and living quarters for Steel Mill. L to R: Bruce, Vini Lopez, and Steve Van Zandt, 1970.

cohorts needed to get to the next level. His surf shop was the perfect rehearsal space, and it also provided living accommodations and odd jobs. He had a great business mind— he understood that artists have to write their own material and hang on to their publishing rights to make money. He knew that bands couldn't continue to play the same songs at the same local clubs to the same audience, and had to get out of their hometown and tour to effectively promote themselves.

To that end, he purchased a tour-worthy truck (and says he still has it). "We were self-contained," Tinker says of the road trips he took with Steel Mill. "If you're self-contained, it puts you a leg up from people who can't do that." Being an engineer, he built a sound system that elevated their live show and got them better gigs. He'd come by his nickname for tinkering with hot rods when he lived in California, but it also seemed to apply as he assembled Steel Mill's sound system. "Tinker is some kind of a genius type of eccentric guy," Tellone says. He "took a bunch of blue-collar guys, put 'em on stage, and made 'em sound good." He gave them ambition to go beyond small dives and play bigger venues, even tour nationally. He seemed like the kind of person who could do anything and be successful. He was making enough money and had all the right resources with the surf business to fund Steel Mill, and before long they were turning

a profit. It didn't have to be much; Bruce said that at nineteen he could live on twenty or thirty bucks a week. It would take a decade before he made real money.

For Bruce, finding talented musicians who were as dedicated as he was, and who could woodshed and travel as needed, was a jackpot. Traveling with the band meant real, albeit periodic, escape, and it grew into a lifelong love of touring. "I like to travel," he later said. "To me, the idea is you get a band, write some songs, and go out to people's towns. It's my favorite thing. It's like a circus. You just kind of roll on, walk into

ABOVE | A Steel Mill poster hanging in Tinker West's Challenger East Surfboards front office, Wanamassa, NJ.

somebody's town, and bang! It's heart to heart. Something can happen to you; something can happen to them. You feel you can make a difference in somebody's life. All I'm trying to do is wake up people's senses and do the same thing for myself."

Tinker was a businessman first and foremost, but he genuinely loved music and looked out for his guys. He wasn't just behind them; he was out on the road with them as part of the team. He made sure they had food, gas, and lodging, sometimes arranging for the band to stay with his friends, as he did on a lengthy trip to California. Tinker and Bruce traveled in his truck and the rest of the band followed. When Tinker became exhausted, he put Bruce behind the wheel for some much needed driving practice. (Girls had driven him around previously, according to Tinker, which is why he never had to learn.) During their West Coast stay, they recorded a demo with the Fillmore's Bill Graham. "Graham offered him a record deal but he wanted all the publishing. I said no," Tinker says. "Publishing is a musician's retirement. I think that should be protected."

Tinker also proved to be an excellent taskmaster. He insisted that rehearsals start early in the morning and go until evening when his surfboard factory shut down for the night. Since he was in his shop all day, he could stay attuned to the band's progress. Critics who say that the "poet of the workingman" never

held a job may not know that Springsteen did a bit of surfboard detailing at the shop, and they have obviously never attempted to perfect the art of songwriting.

It was an art that started in Tex Vinyard's Freehold garage, but Tinker, a musician himself, heard Springsteen's nascent magic as he relentlessly labored at his craft. Bruce would "write songs all the time," Tinker says. "He was writing a song while he's driving. And the songs were stories about stuff. It evolved. Bruce would write these songs on a daily basis; he was always sitting around with an

ABOVE | Bruce performing with Steel Mill at the Nashville Music Festival, Centennial Park Band Shell, Nashville, TN, August 29, 1970. Roy Orbison was one of the headliners. Bruce talked about this gig when he inducted Orbison into the Rock and Roll Hall of Fame, saying he'd spent fifteen hours in the back of a U-Haul truck to open up for the rock legend.

acoustic guitar writing lyrics, trying to make things fit. When he finally got it the way he thought it would work . . . they'd play with the music until they got it." As a craftsman, Tinker understood. Writing songs can be a similar process to hewing surfboards—sculpting narratives out of piles of words, carving out musical arrangements.

Tinker shepherded Steel Mill from 1969 through 1971. They built a strong fan base on college campuses and opened for national acts. But on a trip to visit his folks, Bruce caught Van Morrison playing in San Francisco and had an epiphany, or perhaps he realized that he had gone as far as he could in a hard rock band. Morrison worked a strong current of R&B into his brand of folk rock; that, along

with his horn section and backup singers, inspired Springsteen. Other artists, like Leon Russell and the late Joe Cocker, were pushing rock's boundaries in similar ways, but it was Morrison's live show that gave Bruce a glimpse of the way he wanted to present his music.

Albee Tellone remembers Bruce telling the band members they needed a change. "He said, 'Hey, I need to try something like this,'" Tellone says. "He basically just told everybody, 'Look, I'm done with this, I'm going to start something new; if you want to join along with me you can.'"

"Everybody talks about the Asbury sound," Vini Lopez says. "Well there's the beginning of it, the change from Steel Mill to that band."

It was much more than that. The big show that Bruce envisioned at the time was the foundation of a matchless act that would span more than four decades and bring joy and even hope to millions of fans around the world. It would evolve into "part circus, dance party, political rally, and big tent revival," Vini Lopez says. Fans would call it a house party, or even a religious experience.

"He called it 'the big band,'" Tellone says. "They didn't know what to call it, because Steel Mill had the connotation of being a loud, crunching" band, and "this was kind of a soul band. One day Steve [Van Zandt] and I said, 'Why don't you just give it your name? You're

ABOVE | "Little Steven" Van Zandt was also called "Miami Steve." After playing with Bruce in the early 1970s, he'd leave, only to return in 1975 to join the E Street Band full-time.

writing the tunes, you came up with the idea, it's your arrangements.' He said, 'Well, I don't know, that's kind of an ego trip, isn't it?' We said, 'Do it, believe us, it'll work.'" After tossing around silly names for a time, Tellone says, it became the Bruce Springsteen Band.

Springsteen set about assembling a ten-piece band, but they were nowhere near ready when Tinker got a call for the now-defunct Steel Mill to open for the Allman Brothers Band. The club manager told him, "Give me Springsteen, I don't care how," Tellone recalls. So Bruce gathered a bunch of his friends and formed the stop-gap Dr. Zoom

and the Sonic Boom, which was all about taking the vibe of the Upstage and turning it into a big show. "Because they would be opening for the Allman Brothers, who had two drummers and two lead guitarists, Bruce and Steve decided to match that and go two steps further," Tellone says, "[by adding] two keyboard players and two sax players."

"Dr. Zoom had everyone we knew in the band," Lopez says. "Two of everything: two drummers, two bassists, two guitars, two singers, two baton twirlers, ringmaster, two Monopoly players—Big Danny [Gallagher] and Big Tiny played Monopoly."

ABOVE | Dr. Zoom and the Sonic Boom at the Sunshine-In, May 14, 1971. L to R: Steve Van Zandt (far left), Vini Lopez (barely visible), Springsteen, Albee Tellone and Southside Johnny (sharing a microphone), and Bobby Feigenbaum (far right). A handwritten set list from this night reveals that Dave Dudley's "Six Days on the Road" and Hank Williams's "Jambalaya" (spelled "Jombeliah") were on the agenda.

Monopoly was played regularly at Van Zandt's place, according to Tellone, though they put their own spin on the game that reflected the changing feel of Asbury Park at that time. "He and his musician friends liked to play a cutthroat version of Monopoly for which they would add handmade cards to the Chance and Community Chest piles. If you drew the Race Riot! card, all your houses and hotels burned down."

Times were changing. The Upstage shut its doors in 1971. The same unrest and violence exploding in cities across the nation were scaring people away from Asbury Park.

Bruce had learned to make the road his home, which it would become for much of his adult life. Steel Mill was done, and it was time for something new.

For Tinker, if a business venture didn't make money, it didn't make sense to pursue, and a ten-piece band was a deal breaker. It wasn't "economically feasible" to travel that way, he said. Though he played conga in Dr. Zoom and the Sonic Boom, he had taken Bruce as far as he could. He introduced Springsteen to managers/producers Mike Appel and Jim Cretecos. The next "escape" for Bruce would be from obscurity.

ABOVE | Bruce Springsteen Band performing with vocalists Barbara Dinkins and Delores Holmes. Holmes would reunite with Bruce and the E Street Band in 2001, singing on "My City of Ruins" during *America: A Tribute to Heroes*, the concert for 9/11. Steve Van Zandt can be seen on the right.

RIGHT | Bruce at the Back Door in Richmond, VA, where the Bruce Springsteen Band had a nine-show residency in February 1972.

3

GREAT EXPECTATIONS

Springsteen's two-year *Working on a Dream* tour wrapped on November 22, 2009, in Buffalo, New York, with something the band had never done before and promised to do just one time: play *Greetings from Asbury Park, N.J.,* Bruce's raw but promising debut album, from first track to its trailing notes.

Before the gig, Bruce and his bandmates stood with hands clasped in a reflective circle. "I wouldn't want to be anywhere in the world than here with you guys at this moment," Bruce said. To his right stood longtime friend, manager, and producer Jon Landau.

Standing on the other side of Bruce, holding his left hand, was a man with thick white hair and steely blue eyes. Mike Appel, his former manager and producer, was both an orchestrator of coups that catapulted Springsteen to fame and a litigant who kept him tied up in court and blocked him from entering a recording studio on his own during the crucial year after *Born to Run* came out, his greatest success at that time.

To many of Springsteen's fans, Appel was anathema. To Bruce, on that particular night, he was an invited guest. Bruce had flown

LEFT | Bruce, 1974, in a Triumph T-shirt. Springsteen's lifelong love of motorcycles may have saved him from the draft. At seventeen, he had a motorcycle accident and suffered a concussion—one of the reasons he was rejected for military service.

Appel and his son to Buffalo on a private jet with the E Street Band, hosted him backstage, and dedicated the show to him as he explained the beginnings of his first album to the eager crowd. "This was the miracle. This was the record that took everything from way below zero to . . . one," he joked with the crowd. He told the story about how Appel's "incredible talking" got him an audition with John Hammond, the legendary producer at Columbia who had signed Bob Dylan. "To the man who got me in the door. Mike Appel is here tonight—Mike, this is for you. We've never done it [play the album in its entirety] . . . hope we can do it," Bruce said.

In a way, his relationship with Appel is another one of Bruce's paradoxes. Appel's aggressive tactics yielded vast opportunity while it nearly lost him a lucrative business deal, and ultimately cost him a significant amount of time and money. It would have ruined a lesser artist. Hammond was so annoyed by the persistent manager that he says he was "ready to hate Bruce" when he walked into his office in the spring of 1972 with a guitar that had no case. "Appel is as offensive as any man I've ever met," Hammond says, "but he's utterly selfless in his devotion to Bruce." Later on, Appel would pit *Time* and *Newsweek* against each other for a Springsteen cover story and came close to losing them both. Even Appel himself says he wasn't sure what was going

to happen heading into the week of October 27, 1975, until the magazines made it to the newsstands, both sporting Bruce covers.

It's interesting to ponder Bruce's fate if he hadn't signed the contract with Appel, in what sounds like an apocryphal story, on the hood of a car in a dark parking lot. Springsteen's gracious act in Buffalo almost four decades later says a lot. Alexander Pope, another Roman Catholic, wrote that forgiveness is divine, though maybe it's easier to forgive someone when you've ascended to the highest echelon of your profession and the other guy did not.

But for all his intensity and ambition, there was something Zen about Bruce when it came to inviting people in, letting them go, and bringing them back again. Musicians were a means to an end, and that end was to make the greatest rock albums and put on the greatest rock shows that anyone ever had, and perhaps, like many performers, to be infinitely loved. But musicians were also a family, and like family, even if you take a break from one another you're forever connected. In 1989, he would disperse the E Street Band, only to reconvene it a decade later. Over the years, he reached out to many of the people who left his orbit, either of their own accord or who were asked to leave, with offers of gigs, royalties, benefit concerts, and other acts of kindness and recognition. What fans lock

onto that goes beyond the live show, even beyond lyrics that speak to them and musical hooks that move them, is the realization that beneath one of rock's greatest showmen is a knowing heart.

Appel says that by observing his young signee, he learned that Bruce had figured something out very early on that had eluded Appel. In 1974, keyboardist David Sancious, whose house on E Street would give the band its name, and drummer Ernest "Boom" Carter

accepted their own record deal on Epic, part of the Columbia family. "It really hurt me when he [Sancious] left," Appel told Sirius XM's E Street Radio listeners during a spot as a guest deejay. "When I found that out, I was absolutely bonkers." He told Bruce, "The guy's a genius. When you get a great keyboardist like this guy is, he finds great little parts that make your songs even more magical than they are. He adds another dimension to these songs, and without him, that dimension's gone." Furious

ABOVE | 1105 E Street, Freehold, NJ, was the home of keyboardist David Sancious, the only member of the E Street to actually live on its namesake.

at the thought of losing Sancious, he called Epic and tried to thwart the deal.

"Mike, if he wants to go, he has to go," Bruce told him. "You have to just let it go."

Appel had gotten Bruce an extraordinary ten-album deal with Columbia through his

"incredible talking," or perhaps in spite of it. "The kid knocked me out," Hammond says. They both envisioned Bruce as a solo artist, heir apparent to Bob Dylan, with lyrics that were so good he'd need nothing more than an acoustic guitar.

ABOVE | The look and sound of the Jersey Shore: Bruce Springsteen and what would soon be called the E Street Band. L to R: Clarence Clemons, Bruce Springsteen, David Sancious, Vini Lopez, Danny Federici, and Garry Tallent, on August 29, 1973—the year *Greetings from Asbury Park, N.J.* was released.

Bruce, however, had other ideas. He had his coterie of guys, some of the best musicians on the Asbury Park bar scene: Vini Lopez, who inspired the "madman drummer" line in "Blinded by the Light" (his nickname would become "Mad Dog"); Clarence Clemons, the sax player, his six-foot-five stature earning him his eternal moniker: the Big Man; Garry Tallent, the bassist who would become the longest running E Street Band member; and Sancious, the keyboardist who would go on to lend his brilliant playing to Sting, Peter Gabriel, Eric Clapton, and others. Springsteen and his musicians had bonded playing live together and he thought that with them, he could make the record he wanted. Bruce had a promising future, and now he was bringing his friends along.

There was some debate about what went into the album. Hammond and Appel favored an acoustic album, while Springsteen and Appel's partner Jim Cretecos (who would leave that year, supposedly cashing out his share of Bruce's publishing for $1,500) wanted to make a rock album. Also, the label wanted a photo of their scruffy, windblown troubadour for the cover, but they wouldn't get their way until the second album. Bruce insisted on a vintage postcard he'd found that captures every bit of Asbury Park's nostalgic magic and classic Americana feeling, speaking

volumes about the artist's perspective before the needle even hit the turntable.

In the album's first incarnation, the one thing missing was a hit song, according to music industry magnate Clive Davis, who wrote about Springsteen in his 2013 memoir, *The Soundtrack of My Life*. As the head of CBS Records at the time, Davis sent the album back to Bruce, asking him to come up with something more. Bruce returned home and flipped through a rhyming dictionary for inspiration. "I went to the beach and wrote 'Blinded by the Light' and 'Spirit in the Night,'" Springsteen says. "That was a good call. They ended up being two of my favorite songs on the record."

Dynamic live acts can sound flattened in the studio, and *Greetings* suffers from a bit of that. But it contained the elements of an emerging music superstar: fervent vocals, rich arrangements, rhythms reminiscent of feet shuffling through sand and crashing waves, a sense of place. As advertised, *Greetings* sounded like a lost and dirty weekend "down the shore"—an instant tell, incidentally, if someone is from out of state, because they'll say "down to the shore."

The two late song additions hinted at hit-making greatness. Several years after *Greetings* was released, Manfred Mann's Earth Band would take "Blinded by the Light" to number 1 on the *Billboard* Hot 100; if you

Mission Man, as they head to Greasy Lake for some misadventure. The spartan arrangement is the result of the song being recorded after the original sessions, when most of the players had left, giving "Spirit" an appropriately haunting quality. Only Vini Lopez and Clarence Clemons remained. Bruce played all the other instruments except for some piano by session man Harold Wheeler.

Greetings appealed to the legendary rock writer Lester Bangs, who gave it a generally positive review in *Rolling Stone*, name-dropping influences like Van Morrison and The Band, noting Springsteen's Jersey pride ("Old Bruce makes a point of letting us know that he's from one of the scuzziest, most useless and plain uninteresting sections of Jersey") and his dazzling wordplay ("What makes Bruce totally unique and cosmically surfeiting is his words. Hot damn, what a passel o' verbiage! He's got more of them crammed into this album than any other record released this year, but it's all right because they all fit snug").

were alive in 1976, there was no avoiding the oversized, psychedelicized version of Bruce's song, so prevalent that the casual listener didn't know who had written it. On "Spirit in the Night," Springsteen created some of his most enduring characters, echoed by the backup vocals of the allegorical gang in their natural habitat: Wild Billy, Hazy Davy, Crazy Janey, Killer Joe, G-Man, and narrator

Released in January 1973, *Greetings from Asbury Park, N.J.,* made a ripple rather than a splash. Springsteen was not yet the barn burner on record that he was on stage. He did, however, live up to the music business axiom that you have ten years to make your first album and six months to make your second. In September 1973, Bruce wowed

ABOVE | Springsteen's record label and management wanted him to make a singer-songwriter album; instead, he brought in his band members and recorded *Greetings from Asbury Park, N.J.* in 1973.

RIGHT | Springsteen performing around the release of *Greetings from Asbury Park, N.J.*, 1973.

critics with *The Wild, the Innocent & the E Street Shuffle*, which revealed his growing sophistication in song structure. It showcased Sancious's prodigious chops. *The Wild, the Innocent* was jazzier, funkier, even punkier—more streetwise. The "shore rat" showed that he had spent some time kicking around New York City. It was a long bus ride and a world away from Asbury Park, yet Bruce was keen enough to soak up the vibe of the place and work it into song.

"The first album we did in a week, basically all one take. The second album took more time," Lopez says, but it was also a better time. "There's stuff there that's priceless. Like the yelling in the back of 'The E Street Shuffle.' We have a party going on. We were really drinking and whooping and hollering. We weren't just standing there acting like it. We had tequila, it was fun."

Lopez would be asked to leave the band before the next album. He and Mike Appel fought over money, management, and the ownership Lopez felt of the project. "I started the band, and now I'm getting crap from this guy Mike. I didn't like it. I spoke up," he says. After a scuffle with Appel's brother, Lopez was fired. But during *The Rising* tour in July 2003, and periodically throughout the years, Bruce welcomed Lopez backstage at the Meadowlands with a hug and an invitation to play "Spirit in the Night," which

he accepted. "That was something, going back to play," Lopez says. "Giants Stadium, never expected that. All those years, that was the first time I played with them in thirty years." He'd sit in with the band again at the Philadelphia Spectrum in 2009 and back at the Meadowlands in 2012. In 2014, Lopez was inducted into the Rock and Roll Hall of Fame with the rest of the E Street Band. He probably never expected that either.

Lopez was replaced by Boom Carter, who hung around just long enough to play on Bruce's magnum opus, "Born to Run," widely considered one of the greatest, most enduring rock songs of all time. He'd play it at nearly every non-solo show of his life, bringing up all the house lights to full illumination, uniting an arena full of people every time.

But during the creation of this exultant ode to escape and the album of the same name, Springsteen was tormented by his own ambition and perfectionism. He wanted—no, he needed—for it to be unparalleled. Also, his career depended on it. The first two albums, while getting good reviews, failed to resonate with the public. Columbia had signed a new star, Billy Joel, and was actively promoting him as rumors circulated about Springsteen perhaps being dropped. Moving to a house in Long Branch, living by himself for the first time, he wrote songs under intense pressure. "It was the most horrible period of my life,"

he says. "I was born, grew old, and died making that album."

Bruce and his band were still playing colleges, small theaters, and bars in 1974. On May 9, two days before they commenced the first phase of recording *Born to Run*, they landed at the Harvard Square Theater, opening for Bonnie Raitt. There were two performances that night. The early show was recorded by Michael Atherton, a Boston baker and musician who snuck a tape machine into the venue. His recording surfaced years later and made its way into the Springsteen exhibit "From Asbury Park to the Promised Land" at the Rock and Roll Hall of Fame and Museum, where museumgoers got to listen in to what he heard that night via digital stream. "It was the greatest band concert I've ever seen,"

ABOVE | Sound check at the Harvard Square Theater, May 9, 1974. Bruce was there to open for Bonnie Raitt, but his performance (and music critic Jon Landau's review of it) changed rock 'n' roll history and began a close lifelong friendship and successful collaboration between the two men.

Atherton says, "completely together, completely refined, the dramatic intent clear from beginning to end."

The late show earned singular praise from rock critic Jon Landau, one of the original writers for *Rolling Stone* magazine and a record producer who'd worked with Livingston Taylor, the J. Geils Band, and the MC5. Landau's bold proclamation, one of the most widely referenced pieces of music criticism ever, would change his life, Bruce's life, and rock history. "I saw rock 'n' roll future and its name is Bruce Springsteen," he wrote in his review of the concert in Boston's alternative weekly the *Real Paper*. He had met Bruce briefly the month before outside Charlie's Bar in Cambridge, where the group had a four-night stint. The two became friends, talking on the phone, crashing on each other's couches, staying up late into the night and trading thoughts on rock 'n' roll, for which they shared a clear, anti-elitist love.

Landau's oft-quoted (and misquoted) statement matched Bruce's ambition for his third album. "I wanted to make the greatest rock record that I'd ever heard," Springsteen says. "I wanted it to sound enormous, to grab you by your throat and insist that you take that ride, insist that you pay attention—not just to the music, but to life, to being alive." The sonic elements had to be colossal. To that end, Springsteen and Appel utilized some of

Phil Spector's Wall of Sound recording techniques that they'd picked up from a former cohort of the renowned producer. The lyrics had to be just as enthralling; Bruce says he wrote and wrote and stripped away every cliché from the songs until he felt real emotion. What he was after, and what he got, was not only the success he desired, but something so life-affirming to music fans that it still inspires devotion around the globe.

Born to Run took fourteen months to complete, divided into two separate periods. The band continued to tour during the first phase and recorded without any session players, a somewhat scattershot approach that didn't entirely work. By October 1974, Springsteen opened up a conversation with Landau about the role of a producer, inviting him to sit in on the second session, in 1975, and eventually signing him on as a coproducer with Appel and himself. Landau immediately upped their game, suggesting they move the project from 914 Sound Studios in Rockland County, New York, to the Record Plant, near Times Square, which was better suited to making the big rock record he and Bruce had in mind and a little closer to the musicians who lived down the shore.

The stories of creating *Born to Run* belie its joyful outcome, with tales of Bruce's painstaking pursuit of perfection, retake after retake, and excruciating all-nighters,

PREVIOUS | Bruce and the band rehearsing/sound checking before opening for Bonnie Raitt at the Harvard Square Theater, May 9, 1974.

LEFT | Bruce performing at Alex Cooley's Electric Ballroom in Atlanta, GA, 1975.

guitar player, earning his keep up front by helping to extract what was inside his old friend's head and get it onto tape, even singing the horn parts so that the celebrated session men Michael and Randy Brecker could interpret them on tape. And after auditions so lengthy that Mike Appel walked out of them, Bruce found the right replacements for Sancious and Carter—Roy Bittan and Max Weinberg both played on the album and are with him to this day.

A few weeks before the album's release, Springsteen did a historic ten-show (five nights, two shows each) run at New York City's Bottom Line. Fans got to hear new songs. Music critics and deejays got a preview of the singer-songwriter's evolution; some who had written him off were won over, an important factor in launching the album. The band blasted off each show with their R&B-driven powerhouse "Tenth Avenue Freeze-Out" and Bruce ramped up from there, climbing on the piano and on the patrons' tables in the relatively small, four-hundred-seat venue.

Born to Run made it to number 3 on *Billboard*'s Top 200 and fulfilled Springsteen's dreams of having his songs blast from car radios, which they have ever since. It has since landed on numerous lists of prominent recordings, including the eighteenth spot on *Rolling Stone*'s "500 Greatest Albums of All Time," a place in the NPR 100—"the 100

when some of the musicians would fall asleep midsession. "The album became a monster," Bruce says. "It wanted everything. It just ate up everyone's life." Conversely, the album marked the establishment of some of the most important professional relationships in Bruce's life. Landau proved to be a crucial influence. He elevated the level of professionalism. He recruited talented engineer Jimmy Iovine, future head of Interscope Records, the Brooklyn-raised son of a longshoreman who had worked with John Lennon and done odd jobs for Phil Spector. Landau also provided the right kind of encouragement, the only way to prod a perfectionist, telling Bruce "do it your way, but do it," Springsteen recalls. Steve Van Zandt came back to the fold as a

ABOVE | October 1975: Bruce played a four-night, six-show residency at The Roxy on the Sunset Strip in Los Angeles the same week his *Time* and *Newsweek* covers hit the stands. A star-studded audience showed up, including Jack Nicholson, Gregg Allman and Cher, Neil Diamond, and Tatum and Ryan O'Neal, according to writer Denise Kusel of the *Long Beach Independent*.

ABOVE | At his legendary 1975 ten-show run at The Bottom Line in New York City, Springsteen won over naysayers who thought he'd been overhyped. Those high-energy performances helped catapult him to stardom.

most important American musical works of the 20th century"—and, in 2003, the Library of Congress's National Recording Registry.

Bruce says *Born to Run* was his transitional moment between adolescence and adulthood, and it was, in many ways. The album contains one of the most expressive articulations of teenage emotion: love, lust, loneliness, and, most of all, the heart of teen dreams—getting out of your hometown. Springsteen took classic American themes from his childhood in the 1950s—cars, chrome, girls—and updated them, stripped them of their retro elements, and recast them in a timeless fashion.

The album was also transitional in the shifting of both band personnel and management, with the departures of David Sancious and Bruce's old friend Vini Lopez, and the aftermath of Bruce coming to understand the bad management deal he had signed. "The initial contracts, rather than evil, were naïve," as he put it. Worse—for Bruce, anyway—than being financially disadvantageous was the creative control he'd ceded to Appel, who had "the power to decide all the essentials about how we recorded, who we recorded with," he says. "It wasn't a lawsuit about money; it was about control, who was going to be in control of my work and my work life. Early on I decided that was going to be me." If he couldn't make his own decisions about the

ABOVE | Springsteen performing during the *Born to Run* tour, 1975.

recording process, he simply wouldn't go into a studio, and he didn't for a year.

Instead, he and the band went on the road, making little money as everyone was struggling financially. "We played live, we survived playing live shows as best as we could," he says. "But things got very, very difficult."

And he wrote, prolifically. He moved into a house in Holmdel, New Jersey, that was isolated enough for him to make all the noise he wanted at all hours. He convened his guys for daily rehearsals. With the cloud of the lawsuit hanging over their heads, they began to prepare another album.

ABOVE | Bruce Springsteen taking a break from the sound check at Alex Cooley's Electric Ballroom, Atlanta, GA, 1975.

RIGHT | Bruce Springsteen on Sunset Strip, in Los Angeles to promote his album *Born to Run*, 1975.

4

DARKNESS

Springsteen sits backstage after his August 25, 1978 show at the Veterans Memorial Coliseum in New Haven, Connecticut, talking with BBC2's Bob Harris for *The Old Grey Whistle Test* TV show. Sweat-soaked, hair mussed, his wiry frame is slightly hunched over in a big chair. Next to him is a cassette boom box, a lamp with a fake tree trunk bottom, and a giant can of Hawaiian Punch on ice. Bruce is known for not being much of a drinker, but in his early years he subsisted on junk food to the point where his bandmates would have to force him to eat a decent meal once in a while. His voice is raspy, he is spent. He gives every last scrap of himself during live performances and there's practically nothing left, but his hand movements become expressive when he talks about recording his latest album, *Darkness on the Edge of Town*. "It was more fun than *Born to Run*," he says. "*Born to Run* was really . . . that was really hard."

Caught between his old life and newfound fame, Springsteen struggled to find his place in the world. The making of *Darkness* "was a survival thing," he says.

LEFT | "Corvette Winter," Haddonfield, NJ, 1978. Springsteen always loved vintage 'vettes and drives them to this day. The 1960 Corvette he bought with his *Born to Run* money is on display at the Rock and Roll Hall of Fame. Frank Stefanko, who took this photograph, also shot the covers of *Darkness on the Edge of Town* and *The River*.

"After *Born to Run*, I had a reaction to my good fortune. . . . My greatest fear was that success was going to change or diminish that part of myself." Connecting to his past, he felt, was crucial to not losing himself.

If *Born to Run* was Bruce's commercial crossroads, then *Darkness* was his passage into adulthood. As he approached the significant marker of age thirty, he had outgrown teenage themes, and began to identify more with the adults in his past—the ones who lived lives that he had zealously worked to avoid. "I was trying to write music that both felt angry and rebellious, yet it also felt adult," Springsteen says. He'd also been forced to grow up fast as he dealt with the lawsuit with former manager Mike Appel. The year spent fighting for his creative future cast a shadow over him, and he felt wounded doing battle with someone who'd been so close to him. "The loss of Mike's friendship was a terrible loss," Springsteen says.

A video of Bruce and Steven Van Zandt playing an early version of "Sherry Darling" demonstrates that even with all of the setbacks, there was still fun to be had. Springsteen bangs out chords on a piano and sings, while Van Zandt stands next to him, pummeling a piece of furniture with a pair of drumsticks and adding piquant harmonies where it made sense to do so. When they're done playing, Bruce gets up and jokes about

it being "the one and only performance of this phenomenal song you've captured on tape."

"Sherry Darling" didn't make it onto *Darkness*—it would appear on Bruce's next album, and pop up in his live show over the years. Most of the songs written during the making of the album, around seventy, according to Jimmy Iovine, with forty or fifty recorded according to Max Weinberg, didn't make the cut, but that was part of Springsteen's creative process. "What would happen is I'd write a song, and then I'd write like four songs," he tells the post-gig camera trained on him. "And they would be a progression up, and then the fifth song, that would be like song number two on the album. And then I'd write four more, and like the ninth song, then I'd be at a place where that was like the third song on the album. Meanwhile all these other songs would be transitional material to help you get to a particular place. So that's sort of the way the record was done."

The approach was vastly different than the previous three albums. "Basically, the first good ten songs you write, you put them out, that's your record," Steven Van Zandt says. "Well, that process would end forever." Not wanting to go into the studio until he could do so on his own terms, Springsteen instead became a songwriting juggernaut, churning out material like a Brill Building professional,

even if he couldn't use it. His two biggest hits from this period were songs he gave away: "Fire," to R&B trio the Pointer Sisters, and "Because the Night," to punk poet Patti Smith. "If he thought something was going to be a hit and he didn't want to be represented by that hit, he'd just leave it off the record," coproducer Jon Landau says.

"It's really hard to write a good song," Van Zandt says. "For him to write good songs that possibly could've been hit songs and to not put them out, to put them aside, took an enormous amount of discipline and will-power. It's a bit tragic in a way, because he

would've been one of the great pop song-writers of all time."

Springsteen's "magic notebook," as Roy Bittan called it, was packed with ideas, lyrics, and songs that would be written and rewritten over and over, great songs that might be recorded or not, or wouldn't end up on the record. It became a signifier for the band that more work was on the way. "It was a learning process for all of us, both frustrating and funny at the same time," Max Weinberg says. "We were trying to make a great record. Every time we played we were trying to make something that was meaningful and would

ABOVE | Steven Van Zandt was still called "Miami" when this 1978 photo was taken.

last. We were trying so many different things. Bruce would rehearse us for several days on a song and then throw the song out. He had a plan—sometimes it wasn't as obvious to the rest of us."

The weeks they spent getting the right drum sound alone—including hours hitting the snare, and days moving the drum kit around—were excruciating at times. But Weinberg was determined. Like Bruce, he had seen Elvis on television when he was a kid; only it was his drummer, D. J. Fontana, who grabbed Max's attention. "I think anybody who wanted to develop a life in rock 'n' roll music had a moment," he says. "That was my moment."

The painstaking attention to detail required full immersion from everyone. "The problem was this: I fantasized these huge sounds and so we went to pursue them, but they were always bigger in my head," Springsteen says. "So we were constantly chasing something that was somewhat unattainable."

"We were recording typically from three in the afternoon to three in the morning, five days a week," Weinberg says. "There was this stream of material—and lots of takes. There were moments of frustration for everybody, individually and collectively, but you wanted to do so well, for Bruce. There was a crucible aspect to it: under the pressure we grew, both as young men and a band."

During this time, Bruce also strove to rise above the criticism that he was some sort of hyped-up record label construct, as some critics had conjectured when *Born to Run* was released. "We had to re-prove our viability on a nightly basis, by playing, and it took many years," he says, but his new album would show that *Born to Run*, the record that made him famous, was only the beginning.

Springsteen's copious writing varied stylistically and thematically, but his vision for this album, capturing this period of his life and the world around him, was darker than anything he'd done before. He was after "something like a tone poem" and "apocalyptic grandeur," he says. In the songs, he found a way to honor the working men and women he'd grown up around while working out his own feelings of fear, powerlessness, and despair—sometimes succumbing, sometimes swinging at them like a fighter who's in it to the death. Though he says he was trying not to be self-referential at the time, it's clear from the opening track that he's dealing with make-or-break concerns.

Anyone who has ever felt hollow in their own home can identify with *Darkness on the Edge of Town*: the father who "walks these empty rooms looking for something to blame" in "Adam Raised a Cain," the boy who walks "the darkness of Candy's hall," and the "sadness hidden in that pretty face"

LEFT | After this July 5, 1978 show at The Forum in Inglewood, California, Springsteen gave his first television interview to Eyewitness News' J.J. Jackson (who went on to become one of the first MTV veejays)—it aired two days later.

concerns." He and Landau began talking about creating imagery with the music, "the sound of the picture," Landau says, and drawing a bit from country helped them achieve that.

Springsteen was also keenly aware of the times. It was 1977, the year punk rock exploded, and that had an impact on him as well. He'd been a fan of proto-punk since the early 1970s, when he was hanging out in New York and playing gigs at Max's Kansas City. "I felt some similarity in spirit" with punk, he says. Indeed, the songs on the album were shorter, tougher, more austere, like both country and punk. Even his look evolved. On the album's cover, Bruce resembles a Jersey Shore James Dean in a slightly torn white undershirt, hands jammed into the pockets of a leather jacket, hair disheveled, leaning against Depression-era cabbage rose wallpaper. His expression is nearly as slack as Richard Hell's on the cover of the anthemic punk album *Blank Generation*. The punk rock connection was further strengthened when Bruce gave a song he couldn't finish to Patti Smith via Jimmy Iovine. Inspired by her love affair with future husband Fred "Sonic" Smith, she wrote the verse that completed "Because the Night."

Bruce says he gave the song away because he was "too cowardly" to write a love song at that time. Even in "Born to Run," where he asks a girl to run away with him, he is

of the girl he desires in "Candy's Room." It's a sketch of anger turned inward. The depression that plagued Springsteen at times throughout his life lurks in those halls, alongside the fallout from a year of uncertainty about his own future.

Darkness wasn't just an emotional crossroad for Bruce; it was a musical one as well. He began to look beyond Jersey and cultivate heartland themes. "I started listening to country music, which I hadn't really done before," Springsteen says. "For the first time I really connected with Hank Williams. What I liked about it is country music tackled adult

ABOVE | Promoter Bill Graham held concerts at the Winterland Ballroom in San Francisco, CA, including two Springsteen shows on the *Darkness* tour on December 15–16, 1978. Two weeks after Bruce's appearance, the historic venue was closed.

RIGHT | One of Bruce's signature stage moves that he still does—jumping atop a piano—during the *Darkness on the Edge of Town* tour, 1978.

lookin' through me," he sings in "Badlands." Springsteen's emotional bewilderment is palpable throughout *Darkness*.

Bruce had been incorporating tales of his early years in Freehold into his onstage patter for years, specifically related to his dad, Douglas, and the songs on *Darkness* bristle with that pathos. He'd go even deeper during concerts, describing the bitter arguments between his father and him. His sort of self-psychoanalysis resonated deeply with fans, because he was entertaining, and it always dovetailed into a great song, and he was doing it to heal, not to hate. Bruce didn't want to be mired in his father's circumstances, but he loved him and his family, and he was aware of his parents' love for each other, which is a very hopeful thing for any kid. Consciously or not, he somehow seemed to know that working out the past would give him a better future.

The *Darkness* tour in 1978–1979 was famously explosive, both in the performances and the mood of the band. "It was almost like a wave of relief that we'd been able to stand the pressure," Weinberg says. "There was a ferocity in the band when we finally got out that perhaps wasn't there earlier; it was a take-no-prisoners approach." The album's stripped-down songs translated extremely well to the live show, perhaps even better in their more dynamic, up-tempo form. The raised intensity, the soul-baring rants, a front man

questioning love, and as his fame grew the answer became more elusive. The lyric "I wanna know if love is real" captures the irony of rock stardom and started a thread that would run through his albums for years. You begin a band not only for the love of music but for love itself, but if you actually get there, the motives of others become questionable. Likewise with success and its complications. "I wanna find one face that ain't imbued with punk energy who was jacking James Brown moves—it was a show audiences hadn't seen before. At that time, with classic rock on the decline, it was something they were hungry for.

Springsteen began playing larger venues—something he'd fought against until the demand for tickets to see him became too great—yet he steadfastly maintained the level of intimacy he shared with his fans. "When I'm onstage, I'm almost—I'm half in the audience and I'm half onstage," he says. "And it's really more of a one-on-one level. Like I see the crowd as a crowd but I also see them as like a one-on-one level."

Though Bruce's star continued to rise, *Darkness on the Edge of Town* was more of a critical hit than a commercial one, but he'd laid the groundwork for his first number 1 album. A few of the songs he'd cast off because they didn't fit *Darkness*'s theme landed on his next album, 1980's *The River*. Eight years after signing with Columbia Records, Springsteen finally landed the number 1 spot on *Billboard*'s Top 200 album chart. For the sake of context, it's worth noting that he bumped Barbra Streisand's *Guilty* out of the top spot and was himself replaced by Kenny Rogers's *Greatest Hits* a month later. The state of pop music at the time was such that a major rock act could achieve everything except for chart-topping success. *The River*,

however, was Bruce's turning point, a sprawling double disc packed full of radio-ready hits nestled between tempered ballads. He'd score ten more number 1 albums over the next three and a half decades.

Springsteen became even more prolific during sessions for *The River*, yielding "about ninety" songs, he says, and leaving behind a treasure trove of unreleased material. He had wrestled with the idea that the many styles of music he was making were at odds with one another, only to come to the conclusion that he could and would embrace them all and still create a coherent album. He says the album also set the template for his future endeavors, which would range from low-key recordings to global rock mega-hits.

The downhearted title track was family-inspired. Bruce observed the struggles of his sister Virginia, who'd gotten pregnant and married her high school boyfriend, and wove them into a cautionary tale: a joyless shotgun wedding, a desolate marriage, unsteady work as a laborer, being tormented by lost youth. "Those memories come back to haunt me / They haunt me like a curse / Is a dream a lie if it don't come true / Or is it something worse," he sings in "The River." He made another existential crisis sound uplifting in "Hungry Heart," a song he originally wrote for the Ramones, a band that shared his childhood immersion in 1950s and '60s Top 40 radio.

FOLLOWING | Bruce Springsteen and the E Street Band (L to R: Steve Van Zandt, Max Weinberg, Danny Federici, Bruce Springsteen, Clarence Clemons, Roy Bittan, Garry Tallent), March 1980 in Central Park, New York City. The band laid low that year until *The River* tour kicked off on October 3.

The River cuts a breathtaking swath through decades of rock, drawing heavily from the music Bruce grew up with. The Byrds-y jangle of "The Ties That Bind." The golden oldies quality of "Sherry Darling" and "Out in the Street." The Rolling Stones–like "Crush on You." The classic Americana of "Cadillac Ranch." The Eddie Cochran–inspired "Ramrod." The sepia-toned "Independence Day," another exploration of the father-son dynamic.

Despite the panoply of influences jammed onto one recording, albeit a double album, The River is cohesive, due in large part to the E Street Band. They played together on most of Born to Run, Darkness on the Edge of Town, and The River and became such a tight unit that it was difficult to imagine Springsteen without

them. Garry Tallent's unassuming, perfectly in-the-pocket bass grooving alongside Max Weinberg's commanding drumming, the complexity of Roy Bittan's piano juxtaposed with Danny Federici's shimmering waves of organ, Steven Van Zandt's mastery of hooks and inimitable harmonies, and Clarence Clemons's distinct saxophone with its clarion cries and lengthy, expressive notes—they all gave Springsteen muscle to match his songwriting and his ambition.

Each guy in the organization was a perfect fit. During performances, Weinberg fixed a laser-like focus on Bruce and had an uncanny ability to predict what he'd do next onstage. His and Roy Bittan's orchestra pit background paired well with Bruce's boisterous

ABOVE | Bruce Springsteen signs an autograph for a police officer, 1981.

74

concert theatrics. Van Zandt brought an element of garage rock and a love of the perfect three-minute pop song. The presence of Clemons and his horn set the band apart from all others, as did Federici's glockenspiel. "You hear a lot of talk about bands being family, teams being family," Weinberg says. "At that time, it really was that, because what we had was our relationships and the music Bruce was writing."

As they embarked upon *The River* tour, Bruce and the E Street Band were so in sync with one another that they had nowhere to go but long. The double album would be a harbinger of lengthened sets, and three-hour concerts extended to four-hour shows. The tour also stretched across the world as they headed back to Europe for the first time since *Born to Run*, laying the groundwork for what would become enormous international fame.

The River tour was the moment Springsteen's class consciousness turned to overt politics. Following the Three Mile Island nuclear disaster, he'd lent himself to the 1979 No Nukes concert at Madison Square Garden in New York City—and by many accounts, was the concert's high point, debuting "The River" there. Though he didn't make a personal anti-nuke statement or sign the Musicians United for Safe Energy's manifesto, his presence was enough. When the tour began, he'd wonder aloud what had

happened to the American dream. And the night after Ronald Reagan's 1980 election, Bruce famously got onstage at Arizona State University and said, "I don't know what you guys think about what happened last night, but I think it's pretty frightening."

Still, Springsteen wrapped up 1981 on top of the world. What's a guy with a number 1 album and the world's greatest band to do next? Making a lo-fi recording in his living room and releasing it as his sixth album would have been no one's guess, not even Bruce's.

ABOVE | Photographer Lynn Goldsmith captured numerous images of Bruce while they were dating between late 1977 and early 1979, but it took proto-paparazzo Ron Galella to catch them walking after dinner at a Jackson Hole, WY, restaurant, February 21, 1979.

5

AMERICAN ICON

I came home one day and asked my mother if we were Republicans or Democrats," Springsteen recalls of his childhood. "She said we were Democrats, because they're for the working people."

As a baby boomer with a less fortunate, blue-collar upbringing and an inquisitive, anti-authoritarian mind, Springsteen found class consciousness to be instinctual. But he was slow to embrace politics in work and in life. "I think I voted for McGovern in 1972," Bruce said a dozen years later when asked if he had ever voted (he had also played a small benefit in Red Bank, New Jersey, for the candidate that year). It was something that separated him early on from Columbia label mate (and fellow John Hammond signee) Bob Dylan, whose writing came out of the "broadside" tradition and was overtly political. You can't discount the era, though. Dylan, nearly a decade older than Bruce, rose to fame in the 1960s, and as such his music spoke to a country embroiled in the struggle for civil rights and protesting a very unpopular war. As a star of the 1970s, Springsteen faced the aftermath—national disillusionment, war

LEFT | Bruce began to appear noticeably more muscular during the mid-80s. It was around then that he adopted a fitness regimen that he's maintained through the years. Above, he's wrapping up the *Born in the U.S.A.* tour at the Los Angeles Memorial Coliseum in late September 1985.

veterans returning to an unforgiving public, and widespread economic misery, all of which distinctly informed his songwriting.

Still, he was pinned with the "new Dylan" tag early on, a classification that has never really worked out for anyone's music career. Bruce bucked the comparison like a rodeo bull. He was a band guy, not a solo acoustic act. He had grand visions of larger-than-life concerts. Dylan was more Lead Belly and folk music; Bruce was more Sam and Dave and rhythm 'n' blues. Though the two intersected at Woody Guthrie, Springsteen was an entertainer first, perhaps provocateur only second.

Yet after the tremendous success of *The River* and the expansive tour that followed, Springsteen went solo acoustic—sort of—releasing *Nebraska*, an album that was likely close to what Columbia thought it was getting upon signing him in 1972. The home recording, meant to be a demo, was a uniform collection of American noir, grim tales of shady characters who live and die in the margins. It was also the bridge between Springsteen's class consciousness and a greater political awareness. "*Nebraska* was about . . . what happens to people when they're alienated from their friends and their community and their government and their job," he says. "Because those are the things that keep you sane, that give meaning to life in some fashion."

Greil Marcus called the album "the most complete and probably the most convincing statement of resistance that Ronald Reagan's U.S.A. has yet elicited," though Springsteen was employing the technique of letting the characters express some of his views in their voices. If he was going for "apocalyptic grandeur" on *Darkness, Nebraska* was post-apocalypse—the sound of a solitary car on a highway to nowhere under a starless sky. The move was bold, intuitive, and contrary to conventional wisdom, just like Bruce himself. Despite its dark subject matter and lo-fi sound, it went to number 3 on the *Billboard* Top 200.

Nebraska "kinda came out of the blue," Springsteen says. After *The River* tour wrapped, Bruce rented a house on a reservoir in Colts Neck, New Jersey, a tony township of horse farms and golf courses roughly midway between Freehold and Asbury Park, yet worlds away from both. He had written "Mansion on the Hill" during the tour and now he'd come back, making real money for the first time in his career, and moved into one, at least temporarily. Within weeks, he had written all the songs that would end up on *Nebraska*. "I didn't go out much," he says, "and for some reason I just started to write." He also read. Admittedly not bookish as a younger man, Springsteen had begun consuming books, thanks in part to Jon Landau,

who turned him onto a number of important American writers and set him off on a lifelong literary journey. The influence of the noir novelist Jim Thompson was felt deeply on the album *Nebraska*. Howard Zinn's *A People's History of the United States*, an essential tome describing history from the perspective of the vanquished, not the victors, enriched

the scope of his songs' characters. Flannery O'Connor's storytelling helped him tap into something darker on *Darkness on the Edge of Town* and *Nebraska*.

"The really important reading that I did began in my late twenties, with authors like Flannery O'Connor," he says. "There was something in those stories of hers that I felt

ABOVE | Photographer Frank Stefanko worked with Bruce from 1978 through 1982, when he shot this photo to promote Bruce's home-recorded solo album *Nebraska*.

81

captured a certain part of the American character that I was interested in writing about. They were a big, big revelation. She got to the heart of some part of meanness that she never spelled out, because if she spelled it out you wouldn't be getting it. It was always at the core of every one of her stories—the way that she'd left that hole there, that hole that's inside of everybody. There was some dark thing—a component of spirituality—that I sensed in her stories, and that set me off

exploring characters of my own. She knew original sin—knew how to give it the flesh of a story."

Springsteen says O'Connor inspired him to write "kind of smaller than I had been, writing with just detail." He began recording smaller, too. Bruce had asked Mike Batlan, the roadie who handled his guitars at the time, to pick him up "a little tape machine" and set it up in his spare bedroom, according to longtime Springsteen engineer Toby Scott.

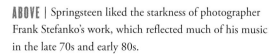

ABOVE | Springsteen liked the starkness of photographer Frank Stefanko's work, which reflected much of his music in the late 70s and early 80s.

RIGHT | Bruce Springsteen in Hyde Park, London, England, 1982.

Bruce's intention was to cut down on the time he spent writing in the studio, a very expensive process, by bringing in tapes of more fully realized songs for the E Street Band to record. By January 1982, Batlan had procured and set up a Teac TASCAM 144, a Portastudio 4-track, a pair of Shure SM57 microphones, and a pair of mic stands in Springsteen's rented house.

The unique sound of *Nebraska*, so suitable to the songs that electric versions recorded with the E Street Band were rejected in favor of the original demo, was the result of a technical comedy of errors that couldn't have been repeated if they'd tried. Simple as it was, the Portastudio was a relatively new machine, and Batlan—who was a guitar roadie, not a recording engineer—didn't have a lot of time to get acquainted with it. "He got some levels and tried to make sure the meters didn't go into the red too much, and he may have listened briefly with headphones," Scott says, "but Bruce was eager to get going, so I don't think he got much beyond the basics. In fact, on some of the first songs they recorded, you can hear a bit of distortion where Mike is still getting his levels."

Batlan hadn't figured out what the knob that controlled the tape speed was for, so they recorded everything too fast and tried to adjust it when they mixed the tracks. They mixed down onto the only piece of equipment Bruce had in the house that he could connect to the Teac—a dirty old Panasonic boom box. "Bruce had a canoe he liked to take out on this little branch of the river that flowed near his house, and the previous summer during one of those trips the boom box had fallen overboard and sunk in the mud," Scott says. "Later that day when the tide went out, he retrieved it, brought it back to the house, hosed off the mud, and left it on the porch for dead. About a week later, he was sitting on the porch reading the Sunday paper, and the boom box all of a sudden comes back to life."

They had also mixed everything through a Gibson Echoplex, a machine that allowed them to add an echoey "slapback" effect on the songs, then it promptly died. Never mind that neither of them thought much of trying to clean or align the tape heads on any of the gear they used.

In the spring of 1982, Bruce convened his band to record *Nebraska*, and ended up recording half of *Born in the U.S.A.* instead. With the finished demo—the only copy of it—on a cassette in his pocket as a reference, none of "electric *Nebraska*" captured the feeling of the original. Much like the test shots that became the cover of *Darkness on the Edge of Town*, this demo was what Springsteen released, with help from adroit studio engineers who were able to compensate for the technical weirdness while maintaining its integrity.

With Bruce's new songwriting process and the E Street Band so in tune with one another after years on the road, recording *Born in the U.S.A.* went comparatively quickly. Though the band laid down between seventy to ninety songs—depending on whose account you're hearing—most were done in just a few takes. The title track was done in two takes, according to Max Weinberg, who says he didn't know the song would reprise until Bruce signaled him in the studio. You can hear it in the song: pandemonium, opacity, Weinberg's explosive drum fill, and the band joining back together for a triumphant conclusion.

Putting the album together, however, was a far lengthier process. Bruce was at another crossroads, and he was having a hard time finishing *Born in the U.S.A.* Success was in his rearview mirror, and the future was undetermined. The making of *Nebraska* had isolated him to an extent from his music family, but he also liked the independence of it and wondered if that was the way to record going forward. What would that mean for the E Street Band—the guys he'd felt accountable to as they all made their way together?

Depression had returned to Bruce, more vehemently than before. *Nebraska* sounds as if it had been informed by gloominess, and for the first time, Bruce couldn't shake it by retreating into what he called his "work

life," as he had in the past. The same hole he describes in the characters of Flannery O'Connor was widening within him. It had led him to a single-minded pursuit of rock 'n' roll glory to the exclusion of everything else, and now that he'd arrived—what next? His loner's pose, the one that had separated him

ABOVE | Springsteen performs at the CNE Grandstand in Toronto, Ontario, Canada on the *Born in the U.S.A.* tour, July 24, 1984.

from others just enough to keep his focus on making music, the one that had given him objectivity so that he could turn what he saw into song magic, no longer seemed to suit him. He took a rambling cross-country drive with a friend. "I experienced a lot of bad feelings," he says of the road trip. "It was an empty, floating feeling, like I had gotten lost. We finally got to California where I had a small house. And when we walked in, I couldn't sit down. I realized that the only thing I wanted to do was to get back in the car and go back the other way. And when I got home to New Jersey, I knew I wouldn't want to stay there either."

"He was feeling suicidal," music journalist and longtime friend Dave Marsh says. "The depression wasn't shocking, per se. He was on a rocket ride, from nothing to something, and now you are getting your ass kissed day and night. You might start to have some inner conflicts about your real self-worth."

"My issues weren't as obvious as drugs," Springsteen says. "Mine were different, they were quieter—just as problematic, but quieter. With all artists, because of the undertow of history and self-loathing, there is a tremendous push toward self-obliteration that occurs onstage. It's both things: there's a tremendous finding of the self while also an abandonment of the self at the same time. You are free of yourself for those hours; all the voices in your head are gone, just gone . . ."

Similarly, Johnny Cash, who lived most of his life in some kind of pain and was very ill toward the end, remarked that once he'd walked onstage, he felt good again, and when he'd walk off, the pain and sickness came right back. Now there were no big rock shows, no tour for Bruce to lose himself in, but throughout 1982 he regularly performed with friends and acquaintances, dropping in on bands like the Beaver Brown Band at Big Man West's—Clarence Clemons's nightclub in Red Bank, New Jersey—Dave Edmunds at the Peppermint Lounge in New York City, Stray Cats at the Fast Lane in Asbury Park, and frequently with an ensemble called Cats on a Smooth Surface, featuring Bobby Bandiera (who also played for Southside Johnny and Bon Jovi), and sometimes a redheaded singer named Patti Scialfa, at the Stone Pony. He played at wedding receptions for Southside Johnny and, later, Steven Van Zandt (to Maureen Santoro, his bride in real life and on *The Sopranos*). In March, he and Roy Bittan flew to Los Angeles to record a song Bruce had written for Donna Summer with the artist herself and producer Quincy Jones. In June, he performed at Rally for Disarmament in Central Park alongside Jackson Browne. That fall, he visited his engineers Chuck Plotkin and Toby Scott while they worked on a session with Bette Midler; in his tradition of tossing off hit songs he didn't think he could

use, Bruce gave her "Pink Cadillac." It later became a B-side when "Dancing in the Dark" was released as a single.

Rejecting songs was becoming a problem as Springsteen, Van Zandt, Landau, Plotkin, and Scott were piecing together *Born in the U.S.A.* out of various sessions. Bruce had written between seventy to ninety songs (again, depending on who's counting) and was precluding some that his team thought were hit material, such as "I'm on Fire," "I'm Goin'

Down," "Cover Me," and "Pink Cadillac." For the first time ever, according to Marsh, Bruce asked E Street Band members for their opinion. The arduous, painstaking process of piecing the album together took almost two years, during which time Bruce grappled with the notion of what he wanted to be, what he wanted out of fame, what he would give back, and how he'd stay true to his core beliefs if this next effort made him the global superstar that his record label had anticipated. Near the end,

ABOVE | As a teenager, Patti Scialfa (far right) responded to an ad Bruce had taken out looking for backup singers—she got him on the phone, but he told her to stay in school. Years later, she'd become the E Street Band's first full-time female member.

Landau prodded an exasperated Springsteen to write a single, something he felt was still missing. Bruce went back to his hotel room and in one night came up with "Dancing in the Dark." "It was just like my heart spoke straight through my mouth, without even having to pass through my brain," he says. "The chorus just poured out of me."

The song earned Springsteen his first Grammy (for Best Male Rock Vocal Performance). Its video, directed by Brian De Palma, with a cameo by pre-*Friends* Courteney Cox, made him an MTV star. Again, beneath the upbeat music, Bruce flawlessly captured his frustration and confusion at that moment in his life and the psychology behind it. "Look, you cannot underestimate the fine power of self-loathing in all of this," he says. "You think, I don't like anything I'm seeing, I don't like anything I'm doing, but I need to change myself, I need to transform myself. I do not know a single artist

ABOVE | Courteney Cox was unknown when she was cast in "Dancing in the Dark," Bruce's breakthrough MTV video, filmed in Minneapolis, MN, June 27, 1984.

who does not run on that fuel. If you are extremely pleased with yourself, nobody would be fucking doing it! . . . That's a motivation, that element of 'I need to remake myself, my town, my audience'—the desire for renewal."

The title track provided a similar function through an even more ingenious narrative technique. Having read Ron Kovic's *Born on the Fourth of July*, Bruce had begun to wrap his head around the predicament of the men who'd gone to Vietnam and fought the war that he had avoided. "Born in the U.S.A." is a powerful and moving tribute to them, but it also mines Springsteen's story, a man at a crossroads, trying to cope with his new circumstances. One of his greatest gifts as a songwriter is the ability to honor the people he writes about while drawing from his own emotional well for depth, and possibly catharsis. Those two songs raised that skill to an even higher level.

From its bold opening notes, *Born in the U.S.A.* is commanding. Its synth sounds and pop inclinations were very much of the time—it was released in June 1984. The album was intended to turn Bruce from rock star to icon, and it did, becoming the United States' best-selling album of 1985 with 15 million copies sold, and 30 million worldwide. Seven of its singles made it onto the *Billboard* Hot 100 Top 10—"Dancing in the Dark," "Cover Me," "Born in the U.S.A.," "My Hometown," "I'm on Fire," "Glory Days," "I'm Goin' Down"—only Michael Jackson and Janet Jackson have had as many hits off a single album. Most extraordinarily, beneath the grandeur and shimmering sounds that attracted millions of new fans were the moving stories that kept his early fans coming back. All his work and stress and soul-searching had paid off for him, not just professionally but on a deeply personal level. Despite his fears, Springsteen was able to achieve unprecedented stardom without losing himself.

The flag-draped cover, shot by renowned photographer Annie Leibovitz, featured Springsteen's much ballyhooed blue-jeaned butt, toned from running and weight training—a fitness regimen he'd begun that he has maintained through the years. Bruce didn't make much of it other than to emphatically deny the rumors that it was a depiction of him peeing on the flag, though he'd supposedly wanted his face on the cover since it wasn't on *Nebraska*. "We took a lot of different types of pictures," he says, "and in the end, the picture of my *ass* looked better than the picture of my *face*, so that's what went on the cover."

Given the album's red-white-and-blue motif, the fact that 1984 was an election year—the year in which George Orwell had set his futuristic novel of an oppressive government—and the let-freedom-ring tone of the title track, it's no wonder that *Born in the U.S.A.* was co-opted by politicos. After attending a Springsteen concert, conservative pundit George Will wrote a piece titled "A Yankee Doodle Springsteen," overlooking the protest elements of Bruce's songs in favor of his scrappy individualism flecked with glimmers of hope. A week later, President Ronald Reagan invoked Bruce's name with an addendum to his stump speech in Hammonton, New Jersey, a Pine Barrens town known as the blueberry capital of the world: "America's future rests in a thousand dreams inside your hearts; it rests in the message of hope in songs so many young Americans admire: New Jersey's own Bruce Springsteen. And helping you make those dreams come true is what this job of mine is all about."

Like the New Jersey State Assembly naming "Born to Run," a song about leaving the state, its "unofficial youth anthem," conservatives mistook "Born in the U.S.A." for jingoism. Requests to use the song, presumably from campaign operatives who hadn't actually listened to anything beyond the rousing chorus, were turned down. Though Springsteen was still a good bit away from full political engagement, he wasn't about to let his songs be used for nefarious purposes. "When Reagan mentioned my name in New Jersey, I felt it was another manipulation, and I had to

disassociate myself from the president's kind words," he says.

Had they paid attention to the lyrics of "Born in the U.S.A.," they would've heard the story of a Vietnam veteran who returned to a country that had no use for him. Had they turned over the 45 rpm single and played its B-side, "Shut Out the Light," they would have heard an even more harrowing tale of a soldier's return, inspired by Ron Kovic's book. The inequity of who fights wars for the United States had long been pondered by Springsteen. In the late 1960s, when his draft number came up, he wondered why his life was worth any less than a rich boy who could defer because his parents had economic or political clout. Boys he knew from Freehold served and died, including Castiles drummer Bart Haynes, leaving a lasting impression on Springsteen. In the early 1980s, he reached out to Kovic and Bob Muller, both disabled veterans, activists for peace, and advocates for vets. Bruce agreed to make an upcoming concert a benefit for the Vietnam Veterans of America, Muller's struggling organization, for which he raised around a quarter of a million dollars.

Politics wanted Springsteen, but he'd have no part of it at that time, not even when Walter Mondale's campaign came calling for help in challenging Reagan in 1984. When asked if he thought Mondale was a better

candidate, Bruce demurred. "I don't know," he said. "I think there are significant differences, but I don't know *how* significant. And it's very difficult to tell by pre-election rhetoric. It seems to always change when they all of a sudden get in. That's why I don't feel a real connection to electoral politics right now—it can't be the best way to find the best man to do the hardest job. I want to try and just work more directly with people; try to find some way that my band can tie into the communities that we come into. I guess that's a political action, a way to just bypass that whole electoral thing. Human politics. I think that people on their own can do a lot. I guess that's what I'm tryin' to figure out now: Where do the aesthetic issues that you write about intersect with some sort of concrete action, some direct involvement, in the communities that your audience comes from? It seems to be an inevitable progression of what our band has been doin', of the idea that we got into this for. We wanted to play because we wanted to meet girls, we wanted to make a ton of dough, and we wanted to change the world a

ABOVE | Springsteen in LA, 1985 on the *Born in the U.S.A.* tour.

FOLLOWING | Wembley Stadium, London, England, July 3, 1985. The *Born in the U.S.A.* tour bumped Springsteen up to the largest venues in the world.

little bit, you know?" Bruce's "human" political action became part of his tours. In addition to fund-raising for veterans, he began helping local food banks and environmental groups raise awareness and collect money at his concerts, no small help considering the enormous draw he'd become. Forget selling out arenas—he could sell out multiple nights at one. In August 1985, he made his debut at Giants Stadium in East Rutherford, New Jersey, with a six-night run. No matter how big the shows got, though, Bruce pulled off the seemingly impossible task of making an audience of tens of thousands feel connected to him and to one another.

"You come out there in that dark, you make that magic," he says. "You pull something that doesn't exist out of the air, doesn't exist until any given night when you're standing out there in front of your audience. Nothing exists in that space until you go 'one, two, three, four . . . whomp.' Then you and your audience together manifest an entire world, an entire set of values, an entire way of thinking about your life and the world around you, and an entire set of possibilities."

ABOVE | *Born in the U.S.A.* tour in London, England, 1984. The physicality of Springsteen's performances seems almost super-human at times.

RIGHT | Springsteen bringing the *Born in the U.S.A.* tour to a close at the Los Angeles Memorial Coliseum, October 1985.

RIGHT | Bruce Springsteen during a sound check for a concert in Kyoto, Japan, April 1985.

6

SECOND SKIN

On *The River*'s "I Wanna Marry You," Bruce Springsteen sees a single mom walking around the neighborhood with her kids and imagines having a relationship with her. He treats the subject of love the same way he has dealt with all the other facets of working-class life—with a dark pragmatism and an occasional scrap of hope.

As Bruce himself points out, he was not big on writing relationship songs prior to *The River*. Nor was he big on relationships, though he had girlfriends and said he lived with one for about two years in his early twenties. "I can't

have any women," he told friends in the early days of his career. "I gotta give everything to my music." Though accurate—it would have likely been impossible to achieve his singular place in rock music without absolute dedication—such assertions no longer made sense to him after two decades at it.

"I guess I just wanted to be free to move, a road runner," he'd said in 1984. "It's silly, I guess. It sounds silly to me now when I say it. Particularly because I don't really value those ideals. I guess I see fulfillment, ultimately, in family life. That just hasn't been my life, you know?"

At the time, Springsteen had finally bought his first real home, another "mansion on the hill," in Rumson, New Jersey. He'd longed to have a place for the cars he'd collected over the years, including the 1960 Corvette he bought with his *Born to Run* money, that were parked at various friends' houses. After the *Born in the U.S.A.* tour, he built the home studio he'd wanted so he wouldn't have to travel to New York every time he had the urge to lay down some tracks. Buying a house in his home state was a small step toward settling down after a lifetime of renting, couch surfing, and sleeping on the beach, or at Tinker West's surfboard factory. Continual touring had been a huge part of building his loyal fan base, but as long as he was on the road, he didn't have to settle down or examine his emotional life in any way beyond songwriting. The three- and four-hour shows were "coming out of pure fear and self-loathing and self-hatred," he says. "That's why my shows were so long. They weren't long because I had an idea or a plan that they should be that long. I couldn't stop until I felt burnt, period. Thoroughly burnt."

The deep funk he fell into around the time of *Nebraska* led him to begin talk therapy, which he'd continue for three decades. At first it was a process of "finding some stuff out, then running away," he says. Always insightful and intuitive, Springsteen's emotional

intelligence had evolved to the point where he knew he needed help if he wanted to open himself up. He didn't want the "unfulfilled life" of the father figure in "I Wanna Marry You." Jon Landau had called him "the smartest person I've ever known—not the most informed or the most educated—but the smartest. If you are ever confronted with a situation—a practical matter, an artistic problem—his read of the people involved is exquisite. He is way ahead." Now he'd have to read himself.

Patti Scialfa, the first full-time female E Street Band member (Suki Lahav had joined temporarily in the mid-1970s) and Bruce's wife since 1991, put it best. "When you are that serious and that creative, and non-trusting on an intimate level, and your art has given you so much, your ability to create something becomes your medicine," she says. "It's the only thing that's given you that stability, that joy, that self-esteem. And so you are, like, 'This part of me no one is going to touch.' When you're young, that works, because it gets you from A to B. When you get older, when you are trying to have a family and children, it doesn't work. I think that some artists can be prone to protecting the well that they fetched their inspiration from so well that they are actually protecting malignant parts of themselves, too. You begin to see that something is broken. It's not just a matter of being the mythological lone wolf; something is broken. Bruce is very smart. He wanted a family, he wanted a relationship, and he worked really, really, really hard at it—as hard as he works at his music."

It makes sense, theoretically, that someone with such single-minded determination could apply it to more than one place in their life. In practice, it's not that simple. One thing Bruce had in his favor was family. The same family whose troubles helped inspire his every success could perhaps inspire him to evolve out of his loner persona and into a committed adult relationship. His parents stayed married until his father's 1998 death at age seventy-three from cancer. His sister Virginia, whose teen pregnancy/marriage he'd immortalized on "The River," had happily remained with her high school paramour. If Bruce didn't yet have the emotional tools to move his personal life forward, at least he had somewhat positive examples. Endeavoring to close the gap he'd put between his family and himself was part of his personal evolution.

But in 1984, he was still wrestling with the issue of his unattached lifestyle. "I don't know if I'm a big family man. My family's been my band. I've always been that way," he said at the time. "I think when I was young, I did it intentionally, because I knew I only had sixty dollars that month, and I had to live on that sixty dollars, and I couldn't get

ABOVE | Neither Springsteen nor his former girlfriends, including photographer Lynn Goldsmith (with Bruce in Jackson Hole, WY, 1979), have ever spoken much about their past relationships, giving him one of rock 'n' roll's most private personal lives.

married or I couldn't get involved at the time. And then it just became my way of life, you know? It really became my way of life . . . I'm just not really lookin' to get married at this point. I've made a commitment to doin' my job right now, and that's basically what I do. Someday, I'd like to have the whole nine yards—the wife, the kids."

Five and a half months later, he gave it a shot. After a quick courtship, he married actress and former model Julianne Phillips. It was May 13, 1985, the height of Bruce's rock stardom; he'd just returned from the Australia/Japan leg of the *Born in the U.S.A.* tour. She'd joined him in Japan, and afterward they'd headed for Lake Oswego, Oregon,

where she was raised and her parents still resided. When helicopters swarmed the reception two days later, Bruce reportedly said, "I do not believe or comprehend the world that I live in." Almost two weeks later, Bruce and the E Street Band were back in New Jersey, filming the video for "Glory Days" in Hoboken with resident John Sayles directing at the legendary rock club Maxwell's. Little Steven Van Zandt made a cameo, and so did Phillips. In October of that year, when the tour ended at the Los Angeles Memorial Coliseum, Bruce brought his new bride onstage during "Dancing in the Dark," rather than his ritual of plucking a girl from the audience, in front of a crowd of 85,000. "I'd like to thank all my

ABOVE | Bruce altered his routine of bringing a random female fan onstage to dance with him in favor of his new bride, Julianne Phillips, during the close of the *Born in the U.S.A.* tour at the Los Angeles Memorial Coliseum, 1985.

fans for coming out here," he said, wrapping up the night. "This has been the greatest year of my life. I feel like I'm the luckiest man in the world."

In January of 1988, they were photographed together at the Rock and Roll Hall of Fame induction ceremony at the Waldorf Astoria in New York City. Bruce, in a silvery jacket, collared white shirt, and bolo tie, inducted Bob Dylan, crediting him with expanding the definition of rock artistry and the pop song itself. "The way that Elvis freed your body, Bob freed your mind," he said.

Within a few months, he and Phillips had officially separated, and the following year they were divorced. Neither have ever spoken much about their three-year marriage or how it ended, though Bruce has acknowledged some of what he was working through at the time. "The emotions of mine that were uncovered by trying to have an adult life with a partner and make that work uncovered a lot of things I'd avoided and tried not to deal with previously," he says.

His 1987 album *Tunnel of Love* explores those themes, the title of which hints at

ABOVE | Springsteen and first wife Julianne Phillips would officially separate not long after they appeared together at the January 1988 Rock and Roll Hall of Fame induction ceremony held at the Waldorf Astoria in New York City. "I didn't protect Juli," Bruce would later say about the breakup. "I handled it badly, and I still feel badly about it. It was cruel for people to find out the way they did."

how the promise of new love yields to lack of clarity as it progresses. The album fits like a puzzle piece in the arc of his career, expounding on questions he'd asked a decade earlier—a grown-up protagonist who wants to commit but is not sure he's ready to trust, who's still questioning love and is plagued by uncertainty. The songs were more adult, polished, and reflective, a perfect move after the blockbuster *Born in the U.S.A.* If Bruce avoided writing love songs in the 1970s, he was making up for it now with first-person accounts that at times felt as lonely and confused as he was when he'd wanted to know "if love is real" at age twenty-four. Also, he'd never quite felt comfortable with the image of himself that had made him a worldwide star earlier in the decade. "I thought I had to reintroduce myself as a songwriter, in a very non-iconic role," he says of the album. "And it was a relief."

The tour was just as much of a departure from previous outings. It was shorter in duration—called "*Tunnel of Love* Express," it ran only for around five months—and played smaller venues. Opening night at the Worcester Centrum, around twelve thousand people, including Rob Lowe and Boston Celtics' forward Kevin McHale, crammed in to see Bruce and the E Street Band's first official performance in two and a half years. Outside the arena, fans without seats offered

$500 or more for last-minute tickets, but almost none changed hands.

The shows were theatrically presented, with the band rehearsing for about six weeks at Bruce's local go-to space, the Expo Theater at the now-defunct Fort Monmouth army base. A carnival theme was created onstage as a play on the album's title track, with a barker, ticket booth, fun house, and sideshow banners, one representing heaven, the other hell, with a Bruce-faced devil. To make their entrance, the musicians had to buy tickets to the fun house. Even the song selection was notably different, with some crowd-pleasers dropped, and "Born to Run" presented in a gentler acoustic manner, with an added disclaimer from Bruce that he was no longer "running."

The shows opened with the title track of his new album and were divided into two parts, one rife with new material and tinged with melancholy. The other was more upbeat, making good use of the horn section Bruce had added, which included Richie "LaBamba" Rosenberg (who'd later gain recognition as a member of the Max Weinberg 7 on *Late Night with Conan O'Brien*).

In an effort to "mix things up," Bruce had rearranged the band, placing backup singer Patti Scialfa to his side, where Clarence Clemons had stood. He needed a female foil to present these songs and these themes,

PREVIOUS | Bruce Springsteen and Clarence Clemons performing at the Capital Centre in Landover, MD on April 4, 1988.

RIGHT | Idrætsparken in Copenhagen, Denmark, July 25, 1988. Fans couldn't help but notice the onstage chemistry between Springsteen and singer Patti Scialfa during the *Tunnel of Love* tour.

wistful in the opening set, waggish in the second. Bruce and the band playfully flirted with Scialfa on "You Can Look but You Better Not Touch."

"I'm a coward when it comes to love," he said onstage. "Save me, boys!" Their chemistry was apparent, and during the tour Scialfa went from band member to girlfriend.

When the *Tunnel of Love* Express tour wrapped up, the band embarked on the six-week, twenty-date Human Rights Now! international tour benefiting Amnesty International. Dedicated to raising awareness

of the fortieth anniversary of the Universal Declaration of Human Rights, the concerts had Bruce and the E Street Band on the road with Sting, Peter Gabriel, Tracy Chapman, Youssou N'Dour, and artists from each country they visited. Even Roy Orbison, whom Springsteen had inducted into the Rock and Roll Hall of Fame the year before (and who would pass away just a few months later), made a cameo appearance when the tour came to Oakland, California. Traveling together with few conveniences through the countries of Costa Rica, India, Zimbabwe,

ABOVE | Tracy Chapman, Sting, and Bruce Springsteen sing together at JFK Stadium in Philadelphia, PA, September 1988.

RIGHT | Taking time to do some writing in Athens, Attica, Greece, October 1988. The Amnesty International Human Rights Now! world tour in Athens gave Bruce a chance to expand his musical horizons.

and the Ivory Coast, the musicians involved developed tremendous camaraderie on and off stage. E Street guitarist Nils Lofgren says he played basketball with Branford Marsalis, and that Roy Bittan trumped almost everyone at Ping-Pong. Sting joined Bruce on "The River," and Bruce sang "Every Breath You Take" with him in return. Fans who observed Springsteen interacting with different artists and guessed that he might be ready for something new were correct.

As Springsteen began to think of finally having a family of his own, he was distancing himself from his music family. *Tunnel of Love* doesn't just reflect his personal life; it also traces his detaching from the E Street Band. They played on only parts of it, replaced in other parts by drum machines and synthesizers. The tour to support it and Human Rights Now! would be their swan song for a decade. In 1989, Springsteen made the difficult phone calls to each member, with varying degrees of acquiescence. Clemons felt anger, while Weinberg says he wasn't surprised; the signs had been there for quite a while. "We stopped playing together for ten years," Bruce says,

ABOVE | Springsteen on the Amnesty International Human Rights Now! tour in 1988, which also featured Sting, Peter Gabriel, Tracy Chapman, Youssou N'Dour, and local guest artists.

"partially because I had run out of ideas as to exactly where to take the band next but also, I think people were a little tired of one another. Which was just a normal thing to have occurred." There had been speculation since the solo endeavor of *Nebraska*, but after the *Born in the U.S.A.* tour had catapulted them all to another level, it might have astonished some. Who would break up the best band in rock? "He had been doing one thing for a long time, and he wanted to try something new," Van Zandt said. "I don't think it's anything more dramatic than that."

There were just a handful of gigs in the year that followed, almost none of which were his. Bruce joined friends such as Bobby Bandiera and Gary U.S. Bonds at small clubs around the Jersey Shore. He sat in with Jimmy Cliff, and with Ringo Starr and his All-Starr Band, which now contained Nils Lofgren and Clarence Clemons. He accompanied Max Weinberg's band Killer Joe at the Stone Pony, then played at Roy Bittan's wedding. He popped up at a couple of West Coast venues as well. He traveled. He rode his motorcycle.

In late September 1989, Bruce got on a silver and blue Harley-Davidson and set out for the Grand Canyon (or so people would later say), accompanied by four bodyguards—three on bikes, one in a van. They rolled into Prescott, Arizona, and headed for its Whiskey Row, stopping at the historic Palace Bar for

Cokes and then to Matt's Saloon, a honky-tonk haven for bikers and country music fans. Outlaw country legend Waylon Jennings had played at Matt's in the 1960s; so had Buck Owens and Lee Hazlewood. Steve McQueen and Sam Peckinpah had hung out there while working in the area. Bruce went in just to grab a few afternoon beers, but before long he'd jumped up onstage with some local musicians who called themselves the Mile High Band. As they worked their way through an hour of classic, easily jam-able hits like Elvis Presley's "Don't Be Cruel," Chuck Berry's "Sweet Little Sixteen," and "Route 66," and a lone Springsteen original ("I'm on Fire"), the crowd grew from fewer than ten to more than

ABOVE | Local papers reported that Bruce jumped over the bar at Matt's Saloon in Prescott, AZ, 1989 to hug and kiss Brenda "Bubbles" Pechanec before taking off on his motorcycle; she helped him avoid the crush of the crowd that had amassed to watch his impromptu performance with a local band.

a hundred. When fans began to mob Bruce, he jumped over the bar and posed for photos with tattooed, Harley-gear-attired bartender/biker Brenda "Bubbles" Pechanec before running across the street, climbing back on the bike, and motoring down Montezuma Street. Bubbles had recently gotten married for the eighth time in a biker wedding ceremony conducted by a reverend named "Catfish." She had also racked up six figures' worth of medical bills, having fought cancer the previous year. Bruce later paid off her debt.

Springsteen admits he was in a dark place during the post–*Tunnel of Love* period in his life and was not easy to be around as he built his relationship with Patti Scialfa. "She had a very sure eye for all of my bullshit," he says. "She recognized it. She was able to call me on it. I had become a master manipulator. You know, 'Oh, I'm going out of the house for a little while, and I'm going down . . .' I always had a way of moving off, moving away, moving back and creating distance." Scialfa also recognized that he was suffering from depression—she says she'd experienced it herself—and knew how to handle him. "I felt very akin to him," she says.

There was a deep connection between the two. Scialfa loved music and had made it her life, from writing songs as a teenager to touring with Southside Johnny to singing on the Rolling Stones' *Dirty Work* album. She

was also a Jersey Shore girl. Having grown up in Deal, a good bit more posh than Bruce's blue-collar hometown, she nonetheless came to Asbury Park for fun and music. Friends remember her as the quintessential rock chick, driving around town in a muscle car with the radio cranked up. She'd even spoken with Springsteen on the phone once, responding to an ad in the *Asbury Park Press* looking for a singer for a "touring band, must be able to travel." She was fifteen; he sweetly suggested that she stay in school.

Scialfa did, enrolling in University of Miami's renowned jazz conservatory at the Frost School of Music, the only woman in her class. She sent demos to record labels and for a time had interest from Jerry Wexler at Atlantic, who had wooed Aretha Franklin to his label from Columbia, and had worked with numerous other music greats. Scialfa moved back north, to Manhattan, continuing her studies at New York University, where she earned a music degree. Living in the city, she waitressed and busked on the street with friends (future E Street associates Soozie Tyrell and Lisa Lowell), sometimes dressing up in cocktail attire for effect.

Though she was a rock chick, a girl who could hang with the boys, there was and still is something graceful, even matriarchal, about Scialfa. When she was inducted into the Rock and Roll Hall of Fame in 2014 with the rest

RIGHT | Bruce Springsteen and Patti Scialfa performing in front of about 150,000 fans at East Berlin's Weissensee cycling track on July 19, 1988. East Germany called it the "Concert for Nicaragua." In response, Bruce spoke to the crowd in German about hoping "all barriers" would one day be torn down as he introduced the song "Chimes of Freedom."

of the E Street Band, as she thanked her three children and her husband, those qualities were still evident. If Bruce was going to have the family he wanted, it seems he couldn't have found someone who was more right.

He and Patti moved to New York City for a time, but city life wasn't for him. So they headed west, like his parents had done two decades earlier, albeit with vastly greater resources, settling into a $13 million home in Beverly Hills. "People always came west to re-find themselves or to re-create themselves in some fashion," he says. "This is the town of re-creation, mostly in some distorted way, but the raw material is here, it's just what you make it. I like the geography, I like the desert and a half hour from my house you're in the San Gabriel Mountains where there's a hundred miles and one store. It was just a good place to make a new start, and for Patti and I to find each other and find ourselves and have our babies." Evan James Springsteen was born in 1990, followed by Jessica in 1991 and Sam in 1994.

Babies and commitment brought about a different sort of creative inspiration. It took Bruce almost two years to complete his ninth album, *Human Touch*, but he says it still felt unfinished at the time. "It was nine months after my [first] son was born," he says. "I was a father, and I had a real relationship with Patti, which was something that had evaded me for a long time." Just before he and Scialfa wed, he had a burst of creativity, penning the songs that would become his tenth album, *Lucky Town*. "I wrote and recorded the whole thing in about three weeks," he says. "It's just one of those records that comes pouring out of you and they always tend to be more direct."

Human Touch and *Lucky Town* were released simultaneously in the spring of 1992. "I realized that the two albums together kind of tell one story," Bruce says. "There's *Tunnel of Love*, then there's what happened in between, which is *Human Touch*, then there's *Lucky Town*. And basically I said: 'Well, hey—Guns N' Roses! They put out two albums, maybe I'll try it.'"

Human Touch is tinged with blues and soul, heightened by vocal contributions from Sam Moore of Sam and Dave and Bobby Hatfield of the Righteous Brothers. Bruce brought in Roy Bittan, who had worked with him on the song cycle, and original E Streeter David Sancious. *Human Touch* was recorded at several professional Los Angeles studios, and Springsteen hired session players, including future *American Idol* judge Randy Jackson on bass, and ubiquitous drummer Jeff Porcaro, who'd played with Toto and left his mark on thousands of recording sessions (and who died just a few months after the albums were released). As such, it bears the sound of the late 1980s/early 1990s, and songs like "57

Channels (And Nothin' On)" are charmingly anachronistic. The acoustic closing track, "Pony Boy," is the album's anomaly. Based on a song Springsteen's grandmother sang to him and he sang to his first son, it segues nicely into the earthier, more twangy *Lucky Town*. Bruce played most of the instruments himself on the song, recorded primarily at his California home. Though the lyrics are very much informed by his then-newly acquired status of family man, he still sounds as though he's coming to terms with success in his personal life. "I've struggled with a lot of things over the past two, three years, and it's been real rewarding. I've been very, very happy, truly the happiest I've ever been in my whole life. And it's not that one-dimensional idea of 'happy.' It's accepting a lot of death and sorrow and mortality. It's putting the script down and letting the chips fall where they may."

ABOVE | Like his parents before him, Springsteen moved to California to start a new life with Patti Scialfa, one that made a priority of marriage and children (with son Evan James, 1990). His albums *Human Touch* and *Lucky Town*, released simultaneously, dealt with some of the changes he'd made in his life during this time.

7

LOST YEARS

"Now my dad, he passed away this year, but I've got to thank him, because, what would I conceivably have written about without him? I mean, imagine if everything had gone great between us, it would have been a disaster, you know? I would have written just happy songs. I tried to do that in the early '90s, and it didn't work. The public didn't like it."

—Bruce Springsteen at his 1999 induction into the Rock and Roll Hall of Fame

Springsteen himself refers to the 1990s as his "lost years," in terms of his work life, even though he earned two of the highest honors in entertainment during that time—Rock and Roll Hall of Fame induction and an Oscar—and his fans remained loyal. They still camped out for days to get concert tickets, though it was a different show with a different band—the "Other Band," as some called them, with five backup singers and only E Street pianist Roy Bittan as a carryover. The Springsteen faithful snapped up two hundred thousand tickets in two and a half hours for an eleven-show stretch at the Meadowlands arena in his home state of New

Jersey. Bruce's songwriting was solid as ever and his albums sold millions of copies, but they didn't stay on the charts as long as they had before. Critics said success had made him seem "out of touch," and he dealt eloquently with that notion. "I kept my promises," he says. "I didn't get burned out. I didn't waste myself. I didn't die. I didn't throw away my musical values."

The song "Streets of Philadelphia" won him the Oscar, along with four more Grammys and greater worldwide acclaim as the song charted even better abroad. Springsteen had written it at the behest of filmmaker Jonathan Demme, who was in the process of directing the film *Philadelphia*.

Demme, who got his start in film working with B-movie legend Roger Corman, was coming off the tremendous success of *The Silence of the Lambs*, which had swept the top five categories at the Oscars. Demme used his momentum to take on the subject of HIV and AIDS in the film about a lawyer, played by Tom Hanks, who loses his job when he becomes ill from the virus. At the time, the disease was still the cause of great fear and discrimination. Demme had no desire to aim the film at those who already understood or were dealing with HIV and AIDS. He wanted to initiate a national dialog, and utilizing the soundtrack was an excellent way to reach out. Seeking a big rock opener for the

film, he'd asked Neil Young to write a song. In the early 1990s, Young had emerged as a godfather of grunge and had been playing loud, dissonant music with the likes of Sonic Youth, Pearl Jam, and Soundgarden. When Young sent him a quieter, more contemplative song (which he used to close the film), he turned to Springsteen. Bruce wrote "Streets of Philadelphia" in two days, a gentle, atmospheric rock ballad driven by synthesizers and drum machines. It was a reflection of not only Bruce's musical values, but his moral compass as well. The emotion he breathes into a man's fight for his life shows his own stunning compassion, especially during a time when a lot of people didn't want to hear about AIDS.

In the song's video, directed by Demme's nephew, Ted Demme, Springsteen speaks for its ravaged protagonist as he walks from the city's shining towers and symbol of American freedom—the Liberty Bell—through neighborhoods blighted by crack consumption (a wall with "Don't Believe the Pipe" spray-painted on it serves as a reminder of that particular epidemic) and poverty, exiting as a small group of men gather around a trash can fire, juxtaposed against a glittering skyline. Bruce was so moved after shooting the video that he donated $45,000 to one of its locations, Sacks Playground on Fourth and Washington Streets in South Philly. "Springsteen was very, very nice," Ron

RIGHT | Filming "Streets of Philadelphia," Philadelphia, PA, December 1993. Bruce won an Oscar for the song he wrote for Jonathan Demme's film about a lawyer with AIDS.

Petrofsky, a district manager at the city recreation department, says. "He said he could see the work that the community and playground volunteers were doing, and he said he wanted to help. We sure could use it." The playground, with nearly four acres of recreational facilities, remains open today.

Springsteen's ability to convey a character's life and struggles was poignant. The video's imagery of firefighters, schoolkids, and devastated streets against a wealth of skyscrapers underscored the class consciousness that Bruce was increasingly articulating. It was also the perfect metaphor for both the toll HIV and AIDS had taken on its victims and the sluggardly response Americans took to it as a nation. When he got up at the sixty-sixth Academy Awards ceremony to accept his Oscar for Best Original Song, Bruce acknowledged the use of music as an instrument of change. "Neil [Young], I gotta share this with you," he said. "You do your best

ABOVE | Jonathan Demme and Bruce Springsteen during a break while shooting the "Streets of Philadelphia" video, Philadelphia, PA, December 1993. Bruce later donated $45,000 to a local park in need of rebuilding.

LOST YEARS

work and you hope that it pulls out the best in your audience and some piece of it spills over into the real world and into people's everyday lives. And it takes the edge off fear and allows us to recognize each other through our veil of differences. I always thought that was one of the things popular art was supposed to be about, along with the merchandising and all the other stuff. Just wanna say thank you, Jonathan, for having me as a part of your picture; I'm glad my song has contributed to its ideas and its acceptance."

With "Streets of Philadelphia," Springsteen took another step closer to aligning himself publicly with social and political causes. The song raised his own awareness of LGBT issues. In 1995, he appeared with Melissa Etheridge on her VH1 special—he was an influence on her music, and she'd lost a Grammy to him for "Streets of Philadelphia"—and they became friends. "I think the experience of having his song in *Philadelphia* led him to meet a lot of gay people and learn a lot about our lives," she said in 1996. "My girlfriend Julie [Cypher] is always with me when we go to his house, and he always treats us as a couple. I've often talked to him about my frustration over not being able to get legally married, and he is always supportive and sympathetic."

Springsteen's conscience had played a role in his career since its early days, as he'd helped

veterans' groups, environmental causes, food banks, and other charitable organizations. Yet as he moved from writing songs steeped in class consciousness to greater political awareness to ultimately campaigning for John Kerry and Barack Obama, his fans, remarkably, moved with him. Even if they didn't agree with his politics—many didn't and still don't—Bruce's relentless championing of the underdog was something that anyone could get behind. That he put his own money into what he was advocating not only did good in the world, but it also gave him credibility among both believers and those who were just in it for the rock.

Bruce's growing political consciousness was the foundation of his next project, *The Ghost of Tom Joad*, which he recorded at his home studio in Los Angeles. He had mined deep into his own life with his previous three albums, and "Streets of Philadelphia" reminded him that the world outside himself still required his attention. Springsteen had been a fan of Oscar-winning director John Ford's adaptation of *The Grapes of Wrath*, and later, the book by John Steinbeck, since the late 1970s. Now he was seeing a parallel between the plight of its protagonist Tom Joad and what he perceived as an assault on the Great Society that President Lyndon Johnson had sought to establish. Those political policies had helped build the middle class and buoy lower-income families. They

121

had also formed the political philosophies of his own parents and himself.

Bruce also foresaw the burgeoning Latino population during the time he'd spent at his small Hollywood Hills home in the mid-1980s. As the grandchild of an Italian immigrant—his maternal grandmother—who lived to 102 and never learned to speak English, he pondered the immigrant experience on a personal level as he observed it play out in California, how people arrived, how they were treated, what they came for, and what they got. "If you go to my hometown, in Freehold, there's a tremendous Hispanic influence, and that was California fifteen years ago," he says. "So when I wrote *The Ghost of Tom Joad*, and wrote a lot about what was going on, it felt like 'This is what the country's going to look like in another ten or fifteen years.' All those immigration issues that people are trying to hide right now . . . were all in the news and in your face in the early '90s in California."

Analogous to the acoustic, home-recorded *Nebraska, Ghost* is filled with an even greater sense of desperation. The eponymous track opens the album with a man sitting by a fire, awaiting the ghost of Tom Joad with the growing awareness that redemption is not coming. Ex-cons find futility in trying to live a decent life ("Straight Time"). "Sinaloa Cowboys" cross the U.S. border from Mexico to pick fruit for slave wages and end up dead in a

meth lab. "Border boys" in San Diego prostitute themselves out to men in fancy cars ("Balboa Park"). The album earned Bruce a Best Contemporary Folk Grammy.

Bruce embarked upon a solo acoustic tour of small venues to support *Ghost* in November of 1995. On opening night, as he took the stage at the Count Basie Theater in Red Bank, New Jersey, he asked the audience of around fifteen hundred for their silence. "Thank you very much," he said. "All right, before we continue . . . a few ground rules (*chuckles*) . . . One is, uh . . . All kidding aside and all, a lot of this music tonight was written, part of the composition of it is the silence in between the spaces so I really need your help in, uh, keeping the quiet during the songs." He'd begin each show with an abridged version of that disclaimer, always including a joke. "Singing or clapping will be met by arrest of a special contingent of the New Jersey state police, uh . . . If you have any of those little cameras, please keep 'em in your pocket or crush 'em under your left foot or something, and it is a community event so if somebody's making too much noise around you feel free in the most constructive way to ask them to please shut the fuck up, all right . . . uh . . . Now I got that off my chest (*chuckles*) . . . Thank you for your cooperation."

The tour strung 128 shows along a period of a year and a half, with Bruce taking off

summer and winter breaks to be with his family. A year in, he returned to his childhood town of Freehold and performed at the 1,300-seat gymnasium of his Catholic school, St. Rose of Lima. It had been nearly three decades since he played there with the Castiles. His former benefactor Marion Vinyard (wife to Tex) was in the audience—he dedicated "This Hard Land" to her—as was Maria Espinoza Ayala, the recipient of Bruce's first kiss, whom he acknowledged from the stage. He played

the show as a benefit for the church's community center, which served the growing Hispanic congregation, with the stipulation that the $30 tickets could only be sold to borough residents.

Bruce had spent a small part of 1995 with the E Street Band to promote his *Greatest Hits* album, but toward the end of the decade he decided to reconvene everyone for a real tour. On a few freezing March days in 1999, rehearsals began at Convention Hall in Asbury Park, a

ABOVE | During the 1990s, Springsteen made a home for himself and his family in Los Angeles, CA, only to return to New Jersey by the decade's end.

Renaissance-style landmark rising up from the boardwalk and looming over the beach. The place was on lockdown, but fans stood outside to listen, trading information online, trying to piece together what was happening and which songs would be included on the reunion tour that would take them from April 1999 into the new millennium.

As Springsteen was rehearsing with his old friends, he was inducted into the Rock and Roll Hall of Fame. Members of the E Street Band were not honored along with him. It would be more than a decade and a half before the entire band made it in, and on the night they did, Bruce told a story about the contention this caused. "Sixteen years ago, a few days before my own induction, I stood in my darkened kitchen along with Steve Van Zandt," he said. "Steve was just returning to the band after a fifteen-year hiatus and he was petitioning me to push the Hall of Fame to induct all of us together. I listened, and the Hall of Fame had its rules, and I was proud of my independence. We hadn't played together in ten years, we were somewhat estranged, we were just taking the first small steps over re-forming. We didn't know what the future would bring. And perhaps the shadows of some of the old grudges held some sway. It was a conundrum, as we've never quite been fish nor fowl. And Steve was quiet, but persistent. And at the end of our conversation, he just said, 'Yeah, I understand. But Bruce Springsteen and the E Street Band—that's the legend.'"

LEFT | Onstage during *The Ghost of Tom Joad* tour, December 1995. Springsteen opened each show by asking the audience to stay quiet during the performance by saying "part of the composition of it is the silence in between the spaces."

ABOVE | The 14th Annual Rock and Roll Hall of Fame Induction Ceremony, March 15, 1999. Even though only Bruce was inducted that year, his newly reunited E Street Band was there for support.

8

THE RISING

"Well, I'd like my life to be like a Bruce Springsteen song. Just once."

—Nick Hornby, *High Fidelity*

English novelist and longtime Springsteen fan Nick Hornby wrote a Bruce reference into his 1995 novel *High Fidelity*. His protagonist, Rob Fleming, ponders the song "Bobby Jean," in which a man goes looking for an old flame, something Rob considers. In the film, John Cusack, as the Americanized Rob Gordon, conjures Bruce himself. Rob lies alone on his bed, contemplating making contact with his "top five" ex-girlfriends to try to figure out where the relationships had gone awry, and holds an imaginary conversation with Springsteen.

Encouraging Rob to follow the path of the character in "Bobby Jean," Bruce casually riffs on the blues, Telecaster in his lap, Fender Twin behind him. "That's what you're looking for, to get ready to start again, it'd be good for you. Say a final good luck and goodbye to your all-time top five," he says with a sly reference to the lyrics in his song. Springsteen seemed fatherly, or at least big

brotherly, offering wisdom and clarity in the midst of confusion.

Of course, his loyal fan base knows this. They view him as someone who can reassure them during turbulent moments— angst-ridden teen years, confused hearts, family rifts, broken marriages, times of loss. They show up at his concerts with handmade signs sharing personal joys and sorrows: "I GRADUATED TODAY." "YOU SAVED THIS JER-SEY GIRL'S LIFE." "THIS LESBIAN HAS BETTER DAYS WHEN SHE HEARS BRUCE." They attend shows for years hoping for the possibility of an onstage hug. They have important conversations with him in their heads, just like Rob does in *High Fidelity*.

In 2000, when the movie was released, Bruce was on the upswing after a relatively quiet period. The reunion tour was on the road, not to promote any particular album but to bring a rolling rock 'n' roll revival to fans in a year when the top-selling artists

ABOVE | The last leg of the *Born in the U.S.A.* tour kicks off before a sold-out crowd at RFK Memorial Stadium in Washington, DC, on August 6, 1985. Bruce told the story of jumping the wall at Graceland and knocking on Elvis's door before launching into "Can't Help Falling in Love" at this show.

were 'N SYNC, Eminem, and Britney Spears. Grunge was over. 'N SYNC sold 2.4 million copies of *No Strings Attached* in its first week, just overlapping the ascent of Napster, which would unravel the paradigm that allowed artists album sales at those heights. It was a bleak time for rock music, and by March of 2000, it was a bleak time to have been born in the U.S.A. period, with a stock market crash and layoffs rippling through the country.

Whether it was his keen sense for detecting cultural moments, his instinct to diverge from music industry trends, or just a desire to rock again, Springsteen delivered what rock fans needed at the time. As he played the preacher, his onstage patter became an outpouring of the life-affirming salvation that rock 'n' roll could deliver. In the HBO *Reunion Tour* special recorded at Madison Square Garden, his face fills with joy as he dances and shuffles his way around the stage, guitar flung across his back, Steven Van Zandt casting amused and knowing glances. Bruce looks in ecstasy to be making music with his old band.

"New York City! . . . New York City!" he exclaimed to the crowd at the Garden during his June 2000 ten-night stand. "Everywhere I've gone, I've seen people lost in confusion . . . I've seen people lost in the wilderness . . . I've seen people lost on the subways in loneliness . . . I've seen people lost in envy over the Jersey Devils winning the Stanley Cup . . .

I've seen people lost at the Statue of Liberty, which is actually in New Jersey . . . I've seen people lost in the New York Giants memorabilia, who, come to think of it, actually play in New Jersey . . . should be the New Jersey Giants, baby . . . I show you some controversy . . . I've seen people lost in confusion . . . but tonight we're here on a search-and-rescue mission, we're here on a search-and-rescue mission, if you've been downhearted, dispirited, disgusted, dispossessed, downsized, analyzed, stigmatized, fractionalized, retro-psychedelized . . . controversialized . . . I'm here tonight . . . I'm here tonight . . . I'm here tonight . . . I'm here tonight . . . I'm here tonight . . . I'm here tonight . . . I'm here tonight . . . I'm here tonight, I wanna reeducate you, resuscitate you, regenerate you, reconfiscate you, reindoctrinate you, recombobulate you, re-, re-, resexualate you . . . rededicate you, reliberate you with the power and the glory, with the promise, with the mystery, with the majesty . . . with the ministry of rock and roll! . . . That's right . . . that's right . . . with the ministry of rock and roll! . . . But unlike my competitors, I shall not, I will not promise you life everlasting . . . But I can promise you life right now!"

That inspiration and healing would become critical in 2001, just after 9/11, as Americans grappled with the first attack on their soil since Pearl Harbor. Bruce had moved his family back to New Jersey, just a few minutes from where he was raised, in the mid-1990s, following *The Ghost of Tom Joad*, which put him in the center of loss. More than 700 New Jersey residents died in the attacks—second only to New York— 147 of which were from his home county of Monmouth. Amid the heavy days that followed the attacks, a Rumson resident named Edwin Sutphin spied Bruce behind the wheel of his vintage Corvette in a Sea Bright parking lot. Sutphin says he rolled down his window, locked eyes with Bruce, and yelled as loud as he could, "We need you now!"

"I knew exactly what he meant," Springsteen said later on.

Having made few public appearances in 2001, Springsteen would maintain a low profile until ten days after the attack. With just an acoustic guitar, harmonica, and a few E Street Band members, he opened *America: A Tribute to Heroes*, the national telethon held in three cities, transforming "My City of Ruins," a rumination on the capricious fortunes of Asbury Park, into part of a song cycle that would help heal a wounded nation. Sitting in the seat of loss, he played a number of benefit shows for victims' families, including one put together by Garry Tallent in Red Bank.

He'd begun some of the material for *The Rising* in the late 1990s, but the songs

acquired a new purpose in the wake of the attacks. Springsteen's father passed away in 1998, and some of the songs were imbued with a sense of loss that translated to the grieving people were experiencing everywhere.

"On the reunion tour with the band, I wrote a song called 'Land of Hope and Dreams' and said, 'Well, that's as good of a song as any of my other songs,'" he says. "It could've been the last song on *Darkness on the Edge of Town*. It could've been on *The River*. It had the power. We closed the show with it every night on that tour. Towards the end of the tour, I wrote 'American Skin (41 Shots).' . . . It gave me the confidence that I could continue to write for the band. The band had work to do to expand its influence, its power, whatever small bit of culture-shaping you can do with rock music."

But when he entered the studio to make a full E Street Band album for the first time since *Born in the U.S.A.*, coaxing a studio sound that satisfied Bruce after a year and a half on the road proved elusive. Springsteen says he'd lost his "rock voice." He would find it with Brendan O'Brien, who'd produced Rage Against the Machine and Pearl Jam, among others. "We got together, I think we did 'Into the Fire,' and he said, 'Go home and write some more of those.'"

Bruce reached out to some families who had lost loved ones in the Twin Towers.

Moved by the obituaries he'd read, he called 9/11 widows and talked with them at length, inviting them to concerts as his guest. "When you're putting yourself into shoes you haven't worn," he says, "you have to be very . . . just very thoughtful." One call was to Stacey Farrelly, who says she was "heavily medicated" and grieving for husband Joe, a firefighter with Manhattan Engine Co. 4, when she heard from Bruce. "I got through Joe's memorial and a good month and a half on that phone call," she recalls.

Another, Suzanne Berger, lost her husband, Jim, a senior vice president at Aon Consulting, who'd ushered coworkers to the elevators but kept going back around his office on the 101st floor of the south tower to make sure he'd gotten everyone out. Bruce called her when he saw in Jim's obituary that he'd been a fan; he also sent a taped message and a song for his memorial. "He said, 'I want to respect your privacy, but I just want you to know that I was very touched, and I want to know more about your husband,'"

ABOVE | When Bruce put the E Street Band back together, he didn't worry about which guitarist to bring along—he brought them all. L to R: Nils Lofgren, Bruce Springsteen, Steven Van Zandt, and Garry Tallent (back) performing in the UK during the reunion tour, May 1999.

Berger says. "He wanted to hear Jim's story, so I told him."

The Rising connects to Springsteen's past as well, utilizing more overt religious symbolism, perhaps necessary to write about such an overwhelming tragedy. His skill for decoding huge emotions is especially poignant here as he relays the vast sense of loss in the small details of the lives of those left behind. Following the timeline of his characters, it stands to reason that some of them, or perhaps their kids, would've been among the firefighters or cops who perished in the Twin Towers. His "Mary" character, a name he's invoked repeatedly since his first album, is back as well, appearing in a garden, perhaps as a widow, perhaps an epiphany, and in the title of another song. "It's not necessarily the same person," he says, "and there's a little continuum that occurs for the people who are watching or listening. The name drifts through your body of work and leaves a trail of its own about where you've been and where you're going." Even Brendan O'Brien, the producer who helped guide Bruce into a new era, played glockenspiel on the album, a ringing hallmark of his work since his early days.

The Rising struck exactly the right tone, accomplishing the near impossible task of writing a response to 9/11 that was empathetic without being maudlin, and was never nationalistic. The album had the right balance of tragedy, fury, love, faith, and healing. "The words felt like secrets told," said one 9/11 widow. Springsteen had actively sought to get into the skin of his characters on the album and the result was compelling. His first number 1 *Billboard* album since 1995's *Greatest Hits*, it sold 525,000 copies in its first week—a career high for him. It also garnered three Grammys and launched the third act of his career, giving him a firm foothold in the new millennium.

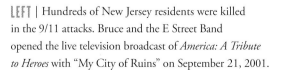

LEFT | Hundreds of New Jersey residents were killed in the 9/11 attacks. Bruce and the E Street Band opened the live television broadcast of *America: A Tribute to Heroes* with "My City of Ruins" on September 21, 2001.

ABOVE | NBC's *Today* took their show on the road on July 30, 2002, sending Matt Lauer and Katie Couric to Asbury Park's Convention Hall for a live broadcast of a Bruce and the E Street Band concert.

9

AMERICAN SKIN

Chris Christie, New Jersey's tough-talking new-millennium Republican governor, famously loves Bruce Springsteen. Bruce, just as famously, does not love him back.

Christie may have been born to run for office in Springsteen's and his home state, but his fandom of Bruce is not born of political expediency. It's earnest, and earned, having attended more than 130 concerts, on his feet and singing along, knowing every lyric, experiencing the same rapture as anyone else in a sea of fans. The governor who preceded him, sweater-vested Wall Street millionaire Jon Corzine, left a Bruce concert before the encores. To Christie, that was unimaginable.

Born in Newark and raised in a modest suburb, he'd spent most of his life ascending politically as a moderate Republican in a mostly blue state. He gravitated more toward the right as he rose within his party, but the Jersey homeboy he worshiped growing up remains his rock 'n' roll hero.

"Just because we disagree doesn't mean I don't get him," Christie says. "No one is beyond the reach of Bruce!"

LEFT | Bruce legendarily opens this show at The Palace in Auburn Hills, MI, during the Working on a Dream tour, November 13, 2009, with the incorrect greeting, "Good evening, Ohio!"

Springsteen, however, is beyond the reach of Chris Christie, uninterested in meeting. In a letter to the editor of the *Asbury Park Press,* Bruce called his policies deleterious to the poor and middle class. He satirized the governor's George Washington Bridge scandal on *Late Night with Jimmy Fallon,* singing a "Born to Run" parody about the shutdown of the bridge under the governor, mocking Christie's two-hour apology press conference ("It was longer than one of my own damn shows," Bruce sang). It took President Obama to arrange a brief meeting between the two at a Hurricane Sandy benefit in New York. They hugged; Christie says he wept.

Despite their common ground—shared love of a widely unloved state, Catholic upbringing, strong Italian mothers—it's not surprising that Bruce has kept his distance from the governor. Earlier in his career, he'd steered clear of partisan politics, whether it was something as significant as disallowing Ronald Reagan to use "Born to Run" in his presidential campaign, or as trivial as refusing to meet Fawn Hall when she turned up backstage after a concert around the time of the Oliver North Iran-Contra scandal. Later on, he'd been more decisive about his politics, campaigning for John Kerry and Barack Obama, and publishing an op-ed piece in the *New York Times.*

What's more curious is why Christie continues to love Springsteen, despite the vast difference in their political opinions, and the snubs. Their beliefs in what's best for the state and the country are diametrically opposed. "Someday, Governor, I don't know when, this will all end / but 'til then you're killing the workingman," Bruce sang with Fallon. Comedy, yes, but his beliefs are deeply rooted in his blue-collar childhood and passionately expressed in the songs he's written ever since.

Yet Christie's unrequited love for Bruce illustrates one of the most fascinating phenomena about Springsteen's relationship with his fans, at least in the United States. Even the ones who disagree vehemently with his politics don't let that interfere with their enjoyment of his albums and, especially, his live performances. In an increasingly polemic culture, it's extraordinary. Consider the Dixie Chicks, whose career came to a crashing halt when singer Natalie Maines uttered a single sentence about George W. Bush during a concert.

Even at his most outspoken, Bruce has suffered little backlash. "American Skin (41 Shots)" is about twenty-two-year-old Amadou Diallo, an immigrant from Guinea living in New York City killed by four plainclothes police officers in 1999. Stopped by the officers, Diallo had pulled his wallet out of his pocket, which they mistook for a gun and opened fire. Numerous songs were written

RIGHT | Bruce Springsteen and the E Street Band on the first night of the Asia/Pacific leg of *The Rising* tour at the Telstra Dome in Melbourne, Australia, March 20, 2003.

about the incident, but Springsteen's drew the most attention. He added it to the reunion tour set on June 4, 2000, in Atlanta, Georgia— just before the band headed north for the filmed-for-HBO ten-night stand at New York City's Madison Square Garden. In the week off between the gigs, a maelstrom built, with strong opinions voiced and sides drawn.

For Springsteen, it was a rebirth; he felt it was as good as his best work and helped him transition back into writing for the E Street Band. He says he was making a larger statement about race in America, not trying to attack New York police. "The first voice you hear after the intro is from the policeman's point of view," Springsteen says. "I worked hard for a balanced voice. I knew a diatribe would do no good. I just wanted to help people see the other guy's point of view." Bruce performed the song at all ten New York shows and shot a video for it during a sound check with Philadelphia cohort Jonathan Demme. Rather than shrink from the controversy, he doubled down, adding a song to the set he'd cowritten with his friend, special ed teacher and musician Joe Grushecky, called "Code of Silence," which would go on to earn him a Grammy for Best Solo Rock Vocal. Its lyrics were about a couple growing apart, but its title alluded to police activity.

Just two years earlier, Bruce and Jon Bon Jovi had raised $112,000 for the family of a slain Red Bank, New Jersey, police officer. Now he was being denounced by New York City Mayor Rudy Giuliani and Police Commissioner Howard Safir. New York State Fraternal Order of Police head Bob Lucente called him a "dirtbag" and a "floating fag." (Bruce would later say he looked up the latter to find out what it actually meant; Lucente later apologized to gay police officers and resigned.) The Patrolmen's Benevolent Association called for a boycott of the shows, but few heeded the call. "It's not a big deal. People blow things up," says Natalie Carbone, a New York City police officer and Springsteen fan from New Jersey. "I don't think this will affect what police officers think about Bruce Springsteen. It's just a song."

Three years later, NYPD chief Joe Esposito heard Springsteen play "American Skin" at New York's Shea Stadium, followed by "Into the Fire," his post-9/11 tribute to firefighters, and took away his police escort from the stadium to the nearby World's Fair Marina. But for the most part, the response to the song was measured. It fanned the flames of debate, not hate. In concert, the boos were drowned out by the trademark of his shows, an arena filled with people chanting "Bruuuuuce."

As Springsteen moved through the decade, he became more outspoken in his songs, in interviews, and beyond. His 2004

New York Times op-ed piece defined his personal politics, detailed why he was supporting John Kerry's candidacy for president, and touted his participation, with the Dixie Chicks, Dave Matthews Band, and others, in the Vote for Change tour.

"A nation's artists and musicians have a particular place in its social and political life. Over the years I've tried to think long and hard about what it means to be American: about the distinctive identity and position we have in the world, and how that position is best carried. I've tried to write songs that speak to our pride and criticize our failures.

"These questions are at the heart of this election: who we are, what we stand for, why we fight. Personally, for the last 25 years I have always stayed one step away from partisan politics. Instead, I have been partisan about a set of ideals: economic justice, civil rights, a humane foreign policy, freedom and a decent life for all of our citizens. This year, however, for many of us the stakes have risen too high to sit this election out.

"Through my work, I've always tried to ask hard questions. Why is it that the wealthiest nation in the world finds it so hard to keep its promise and faith with its weakest

ABOVE | L to R: Dave Matthews, R.E.M.'s Michael Stipe, Pearl Jam's Eddie Vedder, and Bruce Springsteen performing live during the grand finale of the Vote for Change tour, MCI Center, Washington DC, October 11, 2004. Stipe joins Bruce and the E Street Band on "Because the Night," while fellow R.E.M. members Mike Mills and Peter Buck sit in on "Mary's Place" and "Born to Run."

citizens? Why do we continue to find it so difficult to see beyond the veil of race? How do we conduct ourselves during difficult times without killing the things we hold dear? Why does the fulfillment of our promise as a people always seem to be just within grasp yet forever out of reach?

"I don't think John Kerry and John Edwards have all the answers. I do believe they are sincerely interested in asking the right questions and working their way toward honest solutions. They understand that we need an administration that places a priority on fairness, curiosity, openness, humility, concern for all America's citizens, courage and faith."

Yet somehow the man who'd spoken to and for blue-collar America for more than three decades was not at odds with his audience. Ask conservative fans how they can stomach Springsteen's liberal politics and they'll likely say something to the effect of "He backs his stuff up." From the beginning, he built charitable causes into his shows and was continuously and copiously generous when confronted with real human need. He is principled, from refusing to enter a studio if he couldn't make music on his own terms to rejecting tremendous offers for use of his music and likeness. In 2010, Bruce accepted an Ellis Island Family Heritage Award from Lee Iacocca; years before, he'd turned down

LEFT | Bruce Springsteen and Senator John Kerry (D-MA) at an Ohio State University campaign rally, Columbus, OH, October 28, 2004. Springsteen had avoided partisan politics for most of his career, but actively campaigned for Kerry and, later, Barack Obama.

ABOVE | Bruce Springsteen is honored at the 9th annual Ellis Island Family Heritage Awards, Ellis Island, New York, April 22, 2010. Springsteen's maternal grandfather Antonio Zerilli immigrated from Italy through Ellis Island in 1900.

$12 million from the former Chrysler CEO to sing in a car commercial.

While a few deride Springsteen for being a workingman's poet without having ever held a job, it's evident that he works all the time at a job few could ever do. He's disciplined, both professionally, writing and creating relentlessly, and personally, maintaining his physique to the point where he can keep doing most of the things he did at thirty well into his sixties. He takes family seriously, with three kids (one of whom is now a volunteer firefighter) whom he raised just minutes from his childhood home so they could be around his and Patti's extended family. He's about community, refusing to live the life of a reclusive rock star. He may have a $10 million house on two hundred acres of prime New Jersey real estate, yet he's accessible, frequently dropping in on friends' gigs at small shore clubs, taking his kids and their friends to concerts at the PNC Bank Art Center in Holmdel, playing annual benefit concerts for the Rumson Country Day School, raving about how a new supermarket in town is his new favorite place. In 2006, he went to the rebuilt Winter Garden Atrium at the World Financial Center in Manhattan to hear a group of musicians covering songs he'd written for and during *Nebraska* and delighted the crowd by jumping onstage to join the performers for the encore. Whatever he does, he does with commitment and integrity—and he gives it all he's got. His audience may or may not have been swayed by Vote for Change, but they loved him just the same.

The 2013 film *Springsteen & I* further explores his unique relationship with his fans. A collection of homemade videos interspersed with career-spanning concert clips, the film lets fans explain the significant space that Springsteen occupies in their lives. It also captures a bit of the concert experience for the uninitiated, the improvisational nature of the performances, the interaction with the crowd, the strong sense of community. Bruce brings fans onstage—hugs them, kisses them, dances with them, jams with them. An Elvis impersonator—"The Philly Elvis"—recalls that he tried for years to sing with the E Street Band, and a video shows the night he finally made it. He sings a couple of songs with the band and overstays his welcome, but a gracious Springsteen ushers him off with the familiar "Elvis has left the building."

So inspirational is Bruce and his music that people look to him for guidance (captured in *High Fidelity*), life lessons, and comfort through difficult times. "He taught me how to be a decent man," a devotee says. The film explains, in Springsteen's remarkable interaction with his audience, his ability to convey understanding. At a concert in Canada, a young fan with a HI BRUCE, I JUST

RIGHT | Director Baillie Walsh's 2013 film *Springsteen & I* explores the devotion of Bruce's fans and why he means so much to them.

THE MUSIC. THE FANS. THE SOUNDTRACK TO SO MANY LIVES.

"Blue Jeans and Baseball Cap,
that was my first image of America"

"I'll be your
Courteney Cox"

"Thanks for
the music Boss"

"What Bruce means to me
in three words?
Hope, Passion, Togetherness!"

"Bruce's music is the
soundtrack to my life"

"Shorten
your concerts"

"I used to hold his picture
up to my son and
say "daddy""

RIDLEY SCOTT ASSOCIATES PRESENT

SPRINGSTEEN & I
IN CINEMAS 22 JULY

share your stories 🅕 🅨 #springsteenandi | www.springsteenandi.com

MR WOLF AND RIDLEY SCOTT ASSOCIATES PRESENT IN ASSOCIATION WITH SCOTT FREE A BLACK DOG FILMS PRODUCTION SPRINGSTEEN & I EDITOR BEN HARREX
CO-PRODUCER JACOB SWAN HYAM EXECUTIVE PRODUCERS RIDLEY SCOTT JACK ARBUTHNOTT ALFRED CHUBB LIZA MARSHALL PRODUCER SVANA GISLA DIRECTOR BAILLIE WALSH
PHOTO CREDIT: JO LOPEZ

GOT DUMPED, I'M GOIN DOWN sign piques Springsteen's interest. "What happened, bro?" Springsteen asks, dropping his mic down for the man to answer. "She didn't think I was spending enough time with her," the sign holder replies. "You probably weren't!" Springsteen says with his distinctive giggle, echoed by the crowd. The young man asks for a hug and Bruce says, "Get on up here," embracing him. "It's gonna be all right," he says. "I got dumped plenty of times myself . . . Huh huh, they're regretting it now! They left too soon! They missed that record company advance," a fleeting reference to his song "Rosalita" as he launches in to the fan's request.

The film lightly taps into the worldwide Springsteen phenomenon, where he's an even bigger star outside of his own country, underscoring it with humorous translation malfunctions. A middle-aged Danish woman says Bruce has been her friend since 1985, even though he does not know it. She envies the "love" he writes about in "Red Headed Woman"—a song about oral sex—saying it would be nice to be loved like that. The song "Born in the U.S.A." makes a Polish national idealize America over his conflicted country, misunderstanding its lyrics. "You are the guide of my life," a young Japanese girl says of Bruce. An English factory worker who saved for twenty years to visit New York and see a Bruce

concert from the nosebleed section is upgraded to the front row by a mysterious man.

Director Baillie Walsh has fans describe Springsteen in three words, an effective shortcut to demystify the rock star's impact on real lives—"hope," "togetherness," "passionate," "energy," and "power" are mentioned, among many others—and directs heartfelt, tear-evoking thanks to him. Most of all, they convey the intimacy Springsteen creates in an arena setting, a talent unmatched. "I felt like I was the only one there," a fan says. "I felt like he was singing for me." The personal anecdotes and messages stop short of being stalker-y, but convey that these folks spend significant amounts of time listening to Bruce's music, and that the uplifting nature of it is addictive.

By 2005, it seemed that fans would follow Springsteen wherever he led, and he had yet another challenge for them: his thirteenth studio album, *Devils & Dust*. Like *Nebraska* and *The Ghost of Tom Joad*, it was raw and dark and performed mostly by Bruce himself, as was the solo tour he embarked upon to support it. The songs, some of which he'd written after gigs on the *Joad* tour, fit right into the news cycle at the time as he once again slipped into character and sang someone else's life. He considers the personal toll of the Iraq war on those who fought it in the eponymous track. He traces the footsteps of an undocumented

RIGHT | Bruce Springsteen attending the premiere of the documentary *The Promise: The Making of Darkness on the Edge of Town* during the 5th International Rome Film Festival, Rome, Italy, November 1, 2010.

immigrant Sunset Boulevard–style, opening with the man dead in the river ("Matamoros Banks")—a sequel, he says, to *Joad*'s "Across the Border." He's a boy whose mom dies, imagining her spirit as a horse ("Silver Palomino"), a song he says was inspired by a friend of his and Patti's with young kids who had passed away. He makes a forlorn, explicit visit to a prostitute ("Reno") and drops the F-bomb ("Long Time Comin'"), neither of which he'd ever done previously in song.

In the studio, Bruce says producer Brendan O'Brien helped him figure out the right way to present the material, sparse and twangy with just enough instrumentation. For the tour, he rehearsed (at Paramount Theater on the boardwalk in Asbury Park) with a few musicians before deciding to go it alone at venues with up to five thousand seats. As a compelling acoustic performer—a skill that got him signed in the first place—the solo shows allowed for even more storytelling from the stage. On the *Devils* tour, he joked about the stages of parenthood, from the time children are small and parents are their world to the teen years when "they think you're an idiot," he said. Ever the film fan, he used "Racing in the Street" to mention *Two-Lane*

ABOVE | The *Devils & Dust* tour features Springsteen solo on a number of instruments. It's named the Top Small Venue Tour of 2005 by the Billboard Touring Awards (Royal Albert Hall, UK, May 28, 2005).

Blacktop, an obscure 1970s road movie starring Beach Boys drummer Dennis Wilson and a young James Taylor (with a full head of hair). He dedicated "A Good Man Is Hard to Find" to slain officer Sergeant Gerald Vick in St. Paul, Minnesota. He dedicated "Land of Hope and Dreams" to local food banks in various cities. He challenged himself by playing piano, which hadn't always gone so well in the past, but he revisited it.

And for just a moment, he edged back into partisan politics, introducing "Part Man, Part Monkey" with talk of whether Karl Rove and George W. Bush actually do believe in evolution. (W. had said he doubted it.) When

his banter elicited cheers, Bruce balked. "I don't wanna feel like I'm preaching to the converted, that's pretty hack," he said laughing. "I got a lot of nasty letters during the election and those are the ones I prefer . . . Lets you know you're striking a chord . . . My favorite was, uh, a couple of boxes of smashed records and a dead chicken . . . I thought that was a nice touch . . . But where'd they find those records?

"We've come a long way, baby," he said, paraphrasing the old Virginia Slims ad aimed at luring women to smoke, repurposing it to describe what he felt were regressive policies. "And we're going back."

ABOVE | Springsteen plays several songs on piano during the *Devils & Dust* tour, including "The River," "Two Faces," "Racing in the Street," "Real World," and "Jesus Was an Only Son" at this show, and plays "My Beautiful Reward" and the band Suicide's "Dream Baby Dream" on pump organ (Royal Albert Hall, UK, May 28, 2005).

10

HIGH HOPES

During the 1999–2000 reunion tour with the E Street Band, Bruce ended each set with an emotionally stirring version of "If I Should Fall Behind," a meditation on love and how it can lag or last. One by one, each band member stepped up to join Bruce and sang. Nils Lofgren reminded us what a good singer he is. Patti Scialfa's soul-steeped vibrato was gorgeous. But watching now, Danny Federici's and Clarence Clemons's turns at the microphone with Bruce nearby were melancholy and prescient: "I'll wait for you / And if I should fall behind / Wait for me."

Both men would pass away as Springsteen bounded into the teen years of the new millennium, Federici in 2008 and Clemons in 2011. He'd also lose his friend and personal assistant Terry Magovern in 2007 (fans at the *Tunnel of Love* Express shows saw him onstage as the man in the carnival ticket booth; Bruce wrote "Terry's Song" for him), as well as his trainer Tony Strollo in 2012. (Springsteen surprised all of Asbury Park when he played an unannounced set at a benefit for Strollo's young children.)

LEFT | June 25, 2008 in Milan, Italy: The *Magic* tour makes a stop at Stadio Giuseppe Meazza, known as San Siro, which holds more than eighty thousand people.

For Springsteen, these losses came during a period of tremendous creative evolution and recognition for him. He was writing and recording prolifically and more effectively, exploring a greater sonic palette. He'd been addressing the aftermath of war and immigration issues for years, but now he was increasingly vociferous about his feelings on American politics, the widening income gap, and other economic woes. His albums kept hitting number 1. He was honored with the Kennedy Center Award. He and the E Street Band played a Super Bowl halftime show that spanned four decades in twelve minutes just a few weeks after he'd performed at the president's inauguration. He gave an inspiring keynote address at SXSW, the annual Austin, Texas, music and film festival. He became the

ABOVE | Boston, November 19, 2007: Springsteen with Danny Federici, who would take a leave of absence from the E Street Band the following day, after wrapping up the U.S. leg of the *Magic* tour. Federici performs with the band one last time on March 20, 2008; he succumbs to melanoma on April 17, 2008.

only artist to have number 1 records in four decades. The hard-rocking disillusionment of 2007's *Magic* and indictment of Wall Street greed on 2012's *Wrecking Ball* reflected the economic downturn in the United States and the banking scandals that no one was being held accountable for. Now, this time was also marked by bereavements.

It's not uncommon for friends and loved ones to fall away as the years go on, but for the E Street Band, playing together would never be the same. On the albums he made after they were gone, Springsteen included tracks that Federici and Clemons had left behind in the mix. But when the group was inducted into the Rock and Roll Hall of Fame in 2014,

the absence of the two men cut a bittersweet streak through the adulation of finally being honored by the Hall alongside Bruce. Photos of the two and a tape recording of the Big Man humming a tune (played by his widow, Victoria, who accepted on his behalf) evoked powerful emotions. That it happened after they were gone was Springsteen's one regret, he said as he inducted all of his bandmates, past and present, in his intimate, conversational style.

It's fitting that *High Hopes*, Bruce's 2014 collection of covers and rerecorded material, is a look back infused with forward motion. He reinvents outtakes from *The Rising* ("Harry's Place," "Down in the Hole"),

ABOVE | Victoria Clemons, widow of Clarence Clemons, speaks about her husband and plays a voicemail message he left for her. April 10, 2014, at the E Street Band induction into the Rock and Roll Hall of Fame, Barclays Center, Brooklyn, NY.

revives "American Skin (41 Shots)" and "The Ghost of Tom Joad." "Frankie Fell in Love" sounds like it fell off the 2006 *Seeger Sessions*, "Heaven's Wall" off *Wrecking Ball*. And he revisits his appreciation of punk rock, hearkening back to the New York City nights of the early 1970s when he'd miss the last bus back to Asbury Park and pass the time at Max's Kansas City, watching bands like the New York Dolls and Suicide until dawn; he covers Suicide's "Dream Baby Dream" and "Just Like Fire Would" by the Saints, a criminally underappreciated Australian band of the 1970s that, like Bruce, added a horn section to their rock 'n' roll.

Springsteen had originally recorded the title track of *High Hopes*, written by roots rocker Tim Scott McConnell, with the E Street Band during their brief reunion in 1995 for his *Blood Brothers* EP. It was Rage Against the Machine guitarist Tom Morello, a Springsteen friend and cohort since 2008, who heard the rare track one night on Sirius XM's E Street Radio and brought it back to Springsteen's attention. Inspired by the suggestion, Bruce added the song to the set list and they recorded it while on tour in Australia, when Morello was subbing for Steven Van Zandt (who was busy working on his excellent TV series *Lilyhammer*). Morello, who'd also played on Springsteen's 2012 album *Wrecking Ball*, says the sessions were so ad hoc that he wasn't sure they were working on a major release. But as Bruce grew more

ABOVE | Bruce Springsteen and the E Street Band perform at the Bridgestone halftime show during Super Bowl XLIII between the Arizona Cardinals and the Pittsburgh Steelers on February 1, 2009 at Raymond James Stadium in Tampa, FL. They cram "Tenth Avenue Freeze-Out," "Born to Run," "Working on a Dream," and "Glory Days" into twelve minutes.

inspired, his eighteenth studio album, and eleventh number 1, fell into place around its title track. "We've never had a recording session during a tour in our lives," he says. "We did a couple of things that I wanted to put down. So that was very exciting. And being with Tommy was exciting. The band—Steven, Nils, all those guys—continues to be a source of inspiration for me."

Morello and Springsteen, with their concurring political beliefs and divergent music output, are the likeliest of friends. Morello, who has at times courted controversy with ideological statements, and Springsteen, who avoided partisan politics for much of his career, seem to be great influences on each

other. Morello energizes Springsteen. "Tom and his guitar became my muse, pushing the rest of this project to another level," Bruce penned in the liner notes to *High Hopes*. In return, he expanded Morello's repertoire (the 2013 tour featured a staggering 223 different songs), not to mention putting him through the paces of a three-and-a-half-hour set. A lead guitarist for Rage, Morello says he'd never sang with an electric guitar in his hands until he first joined Springsteen onstage in 2008 for "The Ghost of Tom Joad" at the Pond in Anaheim. (Rage had recorded a thrash-rap version of the song a decade earlier.) Bruce liked what Morello added to the song so much that he rerecorded it with Tom for *High Hopes*.

ABOVE | While on the *Wrecking Ball* tour in Australia, Bruce Springsteen goes into the studio with guitarist Tom Morello and does some recording that leads to the next album, *High Hopes* (Allphones Arena, Sydney, Australia, March 18, 2013).

Like the John Steinbeck character who inspired it, "The Ghost of Tom Joad" is as relevant now as ever. "I think it was one of Bruce's best songs and it really cuts to the core of his social justice writing in a way that it tells a story," Morello says. "The song tells a very human tale, and the musical accompaniment of the song invokes the very different ends of the struggle for social justice spectrum. There's a plaintive ballad, which feels like a lament. And there's the full-bore rocker that feels like a threat."

Springsteen's humanity is part of what makes his songs timeless, and why they are so continuously applicable to crises and injustice. In concert, he dedicated "American Skin (41 Shots)" to Trayvon Martin, the seventeen-year-old shot dead in Florida by neighborhood watchman George Zimmerman, who was later acquitted of murder. He dusted off "My City of Ruins" for post-Katrina New Orleans when he performed there eight months after the disaster. It was the opening gig of the 2006 *Seeger Sessions* tour, a large cabal of musicians he'd assembled to play traditional songs popularized by folk icon and activist Pete Seeger, at the Jazz and Heritage Festival. Bruce didn't hold back his feeling that the government had failed its citizens, dedicating "How Can a Poor Man Stand Such Times and Live?" to "President Bystander" (a reference to George W. Bush, who was widely criticized for his handling of the tragedy) and including local references in a verse:

"There's bodies floatin' on the canal and the levees gone to hell / Them who's got out of town and them who ain't got left to drown."

It was Bruce's Jazz Fest debut; perhaps he knew the people of New Orleans needed him, and he articulated their frustration and anguish. "I saw sights I never thought I'd see in an American city," he said from the stage of his visit to the Ninth Ward, the section of the city hit hardest by the hurricane. "The criminal ineptitude makes you furious."

Although that first gig called for moral outrage, *The Seeger Sessions* was generally a more joyful endeavor. *Devils & Dust* felt like

an ominous response to a second Bush term. This venture embodied the more positive spirit of Seeger, or as Springsteen put it at Seeger's ninetieth birthday celebration concert at Madison Square Garden, his "stubborn, defiant, and nasty optimism." But Bruce also loved the music. In a way, the project had evolved slowly. Springsteen had recorded "We Shall Overcome" in 1997 for a tribute album and began exploring Seeger's oeuvre. When he put the project together, he called up some folks he'd casually jammed with over the years. It grew into anywhere between seventeen and twenty pickers and grinners bearing stringed instruments, horns, and percussion. The big band was a part of Springsteen's history,

ABOVE | Bruce plays with numerous performers at The Clearwater Concert at Madison Square Garden in New York, May 3, 2009, celebrating Pete Seeger's ninetieth birthday. L to R: Arlo Guthrie, Springsteen, Tom Morello, and Joan Baez. Proceeds benefit the Hudson River Sloop Clearwater, a nonprofit corporation founded by Seeger in 1966 to bring environmental attention to the Hudson River Valley.

after all; he'd assembled Dr. Zoom and the Sonic Boom with numerous instrumentalists of all sorts and had a ten-piece, eponymously named act before he was signed as a solo artist. The album he made with his new conclave, *We Shall Overcome: The Seeger Sessions*, is an uplifting hootenanny, a rocking celebration of Seeger's straightforward, sing-along folk music. The tour for the album followed in that spirit—not a bad way to ride out the administration that Bruce had campaigned against.

In 2009, the man he'd campaigned for was sworn in as Barack Obama became the forty-fourth president of the United States. Springsteen and Seeger performed Woody Guthrie's "This Land Is Your Land" at the inauguration, with Seeger insisting that all the verses be sung. Later in the year, at Pete's ninetieth birthday party, Bruce spoke of the trip in terms of what Seeger had meant to him, and what he meant to the nation:

"As Pete and I traveled to Washington for President Obama's inaugural celebration, he told me the entire story of 'We Shall Overcome.' How it moved from a labor movement song, and with Pete's inspiration, had been adapted by the civil rights movement. That day as we sang 'This Land Is Your Land,' I looked at Pete, the first black president of the United States was seated to his right, and I thought of the incredible journey that Pete had taken. My own growing up in the sixties in towns scarred by race rioting made that moment nearly unbelievable, and Pete had thirty extra years of struggle and real activism on his belt . . . At some point, Pete Seeger decided he'd be a walking, singing reminder of all of America's history. He'd be a living archive of America's music and conscience, a testament of the power of song and culture to nudge history along, to push American events towards more humane and justified ends."

Though a longtime Woody Guthrie fan, Springsteen had skipped over Seeger for a long time, discovering the folksinger later in life, but their common ground was apparent. He and Seeger were both elected to the American Academy of Arts & Sciences' class of 2013—two of only nine in the "Performing Arts—Criticism and Practice" category (Robert De Niro and Herbie Hancock among them as well). Three months later, Seeger passed away at age ninety-four.

Loss was never too far from Springsteen during these years, and in October 2012,

it washed over his beloved Asbury Park. Hurricane Sandy was one of the largest storms to ever come off the Atlantic Ocean. It picked up strength as it traveled north on the Gulf Stream until a high-pressure air mass from Canada steered it sharply to the left. It made landfall on the Jersey Shore, destroying stretches of boardwalk, beaches, homes, shops, restaurants, bars, and amusement parks like the one Bruce sang about in "Born to Run." It

ABOVE | Springsteen performs "The Rising" with the Joyce Garrett Singers, a gospel choir, during the "We Are One: The Obama Inaugural Celebration at the Lincoln Memorial" event in Washington, DC, January 18, 2009.

pushed a foot of sand into Convention Hall, the site of many a Springsteen rehearsal for his worldwide tours.

The damage Sandy left behind was colossal. In the United States alone, 117 people died, millions had no electricity for weeks or months, and it cost the affected states billions of dollars. Floods and fires left devastation. Families were left homeless, and tangible memories were destroyed.

"The size of destruction was shocking," Springsteen says. "It took days and days to understand the level of destruction that occurred along the Jersey Shore."

A native and lifelong resident, Bruce instantly comprehended what had been lost—not just the memories of countless kids who grew up in New Jersey and summered on the shore, but a destination that had been affordable and accessible, and would perhaps no longer be in the aftermath of the storm. "The Jersey Coast had a very unique personality," he says, "some places where there's well-to-do people, some places where there's a lot of working-class people and middle-class people who were able to have homes. So to see it washed away was very painful."

Springsteen was the first to sign on for an immediate telethon to raise money for victims of the disaster. *Hurricane Sandy: Coming Together* aired commercial-free on NBC just two days after the storm had dissipated. Tristate-area denizens such as Christina Aguilera, Billy Joel, Mary J. Blige, and Jon Bon

ABOVE | "The amusement park rises bold and stark." Superstorm Sandy devastates Springsteen's beloved Jersey Shore when it makes landfall on October 29, 2012. The Jet Star roller coaster on the Casino Pier in Seaside Heights, NJ, becomes an iconic image of the storm after it is swept into the Atlantic Ocean.

Jovi gathered together in Studio 6A at 30 Rock in New York City and raised more than $23 million for the Red Cross. Bruce closed the show with "Land of Hope and Dreams," which led into "People Get Ready," as it often did.

An even larger effort, 12-12-12, the Concert for Sandy Relief, was a six-hour event held at Madison Square Garden, featuring the Rolling Stones, the Who, Paul McCartney, Dave Grohl, Kanye West, and many others. All proceeds went to the Robin Hood Foundation, a poverty-fighting nonprofit. This time, the E Street Band opened the show, with "Land of Hope and Dreams," "Wrecking Ball," and of course "My City of Ruins," his Asbury Park lament, ending their set with his

friend Jon Bon Jovi guest-singing on "Born to Run."

For all of 2013 and the first quarter of 2014, though, Springsteen promoted *Wrecking Ball* and *High Hopes* with tours outside of the United States. Since the *Born in the U.S.A.* days, the love for him abroad had outpaced his devoted American fan base with zeal. His 1988 show at the Radrennbahn Weissensee, which was in East Berlin at the time, drew a crowd of 160,000—the largest it had ever seen. Springsteen famously told them that he was "not being here for or against any certain government, but to play rock 'n' roll for [you] East Berliners . . . in the hope that one day, all barriers will be torn down." The following year, the Berlin Wall was turned into rubble.

Europeans have historically shown tremendous appreciation for America's rock, country, and blues. They tend to be fond of socially conscious Americans, of which Springsteen is obviously one. But it's more than that. His audience in Europe is younger than in the states. They don't cling to Springsteen's historical touchstones and thus lack certain expectations of American audiences. Either they hadn't been born until after the 1970s or weren't clued in to Bruce the way many of his U.S. fans were. They embrace new material, unlike those fans who want to hear standards such as "Born to Run." The

economic woes of some of these countries have hit their youth especially hard, making his newer songs even more appealing. And the places he sings about—the Jersey Shore in his earlier work, the Southwest on later albums—are exotic to them.

Bruce says there's an emotional openness among European fans that's rare in the states. They express enthusiasm for him more acutely.

LEFT | Bruce and the E Street Band play the Glastonbury Music Festival in Pilton, England, June 27, 2009. Earlier in the day, Springsteen thrills the massive crowd when he joins fellow New Jersey rockers the Gaslight Anthem on their song "The '59 Sound."

ABOVE | Fans at the Weissensee cycling track in East Berlin hoist a "Born in the U.S.A." sign at Springsteen's only concert in East Germany, July 19, 1988.

In Milan, Italy, he was greeted by a sign that reads: LAST WEEK ARRIVED THE POPE, NEXT WEEK WILL COME MADONNA, BUT GOD IS HERE . . . NOW. In Gothenburg, Sweden—a country where Springsteen-mania puts him on the front pages of newspapers when he visits—a fevered audience caused structural damage to the arena during a concert. In smaller towns, filling a fifty-thousand-seat arena constitutes a huge chunk of the local population, making an E Street Band visit such a significant event that nearly everything closes up for the night.

And the hand-hewn signs that audience members flash to request a song, send Bruce a message, or ask a question are as wide open as the crowds themselves. Springsteen waded into the European audiences almost nightly, plucking the more original ones, from the sacred to the profane, challenging himself and his band to play the requests. In Hannover, Germany, a fan's handmade sign offers a trade for a request: I'D GIVE MY RIGHT TESTICLE TO HEAR DRIFT AWAY, a Dobie Gray cover. "I'll play 'Drift Away,'" Bruce replied, "as long as I don't have to see the left or right testicle."

ABOVE | Outside the Stadio Giuseppe Meazza (San Siro) in Milan, Italy, June 12, 2012. European fans have a special love of Bruce, reflected in the homemade placards they bring to his concerts.

The conversation he began with his audience decades ago continues. "We're here for one reason," he says from the stage in *Springsteen & I*, "because you're here."

After over fifty years of playing music, Springsteen shows no signs of slowing down. He's still challenging himself creatively, codirecting a ten-minute film with longtime documentarian Thom Zimny, a companion piece to *High Hopes*' post-apocalyptic "Hunter of Invisible Game." He also made his acting debut in the season three finale of *Lilyhammer*, playing a mortician and hit man, directed by Steve Van Zandt. Thanks to a dedication to fitness and the luck of a gene pool jackpot, he can still tour, play the epic shows, leap up on top of pianos, and crowd-surf as he has always done. What started as obsession for him is now a calling, and the calling doesn't exist without that conversation. Back in 1985, he described his commitment to his audience. "That ticket is my handshake," he said. "That ticket is me promising you that it's gonna be all the way every chance I get. That's my contract."

It's still a contract, and he's as excited about it as ever, possibly more. In mid-2014, he posted a thank-you note on his website to fans who'd come out to see him on the *Wrecking Ball* and *High Hopes* tour, along with the film he made with Zimny:

"The past 2 plus years and nearly 170 shows have been a life changer. Thanks to you, we have dwelled deep within the transformative power of rock 'n' roll. You've helped us bring a new and revitalized E St. Band into being. We take this break with a sense of joy, renewed purpose and filled with the spirit to bring you our best in the future."

ABOVE | Bruce Springsteen and the E Street Band, including saxophonist Jake Clemons (third from right), nephew of Clarence Clemons, at the New Orleans Jazz & Heritage Festival at the Fair Grounds, New Orleans, Louisiana, May 3, 2014.

SELECTED BIBLIOGRAPHY

http://brucebase.wikispaces.com/

Barnes, Julian. "Springsteen Song About Diallo Prompts Anger From Police," *New York Times*, June 13, 2000.

Burger, Jeff, ed. *Springsteen on Springsteen: Interviews, Speeches, and Encounters.* Chicago Review Press, 2013.

Cahillane, Kevin. "Two Guys Left Behind in the E Street Shuffle," *New York Times*, May 1, 2005.

Cameron, Keith. "Bruce Springsteen: 'People thought we were gone. Finished,'" *The Guardian*, September 23, 2010.

Cannon, Bob. "Springsteen's Bride and Joy," *Entertainment Weekly*, May 14, 1993.

Carlin, Peter Ames. *Bruce.* Touchstone/Simon & Schuster, 2012.

Chrome Dreams Video. *Bruce Springsteen: Becoming the Boss: 1949–1985*, released 2005.

Coyne, Kevin. "The Boss on Stage, but 'Saddie' Out in Right," *New York Times*, July 9, 2011.

Dempsey, Ian. Radio interview, RTE 2FM (Ireland), May 14, 1993.

Dolan, Mark. *Bruce Springsteen and the Promise of Rock 'n' Roll.* W. W. Norton, 2012.

Duffy, John. *Bruce Springsteen in His Own Words.* Music Sales Corporation, 2000.

Flippo, Chet. "Blue-Collar Troubadour," *People*, September 3, 1984.

Gellman, Gary. *Let's Talk* #152, video interview with Carl "Tinker" West.

Goldstein, Stan. Bruce Blog, *Star-Ledger* (Newark, NJ).

Greene, Andy. "Bruce Springsteen and the E Street Band Look Back at Epic Tour," *Rolling Stone*, December 10, 2009.

Herman, Dave. *King Biscuit Flower Hour* radio interview, July 9, 1978.

Heylin, Clinton. *E Street Shuffle: The Glory Days of Bruce Springsteen & the E Street Band.* Viking, 2013.

Holden, Stephen. "When the Boss Fell to Earth, He Hit Paradise," *New York Times*, August 9, 1992.

Hyman, Mark. "The Boss Grew Up Here—But Mum's the Word," *Businessweek*, October 2, 2000.

Keller, Daniel. "Bruce Springsteen's 'Nebraska'—A PortaStudio, two SM57's, and Inspiration," TASCAM.com, July 25, 2007.

Levy, Joe. "Bruce Springsteen: The *Rolling Stone* Interview," *Rolling Stone*, November 1, 2007.

Loder, Kurt. "The *Rolling Stone* Interview: Bruce Springsteen on 'Born in the U.S.A.,'" *Rolling Stone*, December 6, 1984.

Lotz, Griffin. "Bruce Springsteen Makes a Surprise Appearance at New Jersey Fundraiser," *Rolling Stone*, February 26, 2012.

Lustig, Jay. "Max Weinberg Hits the Road Again with His Big Band," *Star-Ledger* (Newark, NJ), November 2, 2010.

Marsh, Dave. *Two Hearts: The Definitive Biography 1972–2003.* Routledge, 2003.

———. *Bruce Springsteen on Tour: 1968–2005.* Bloomsbury, 2006.

Masur, Louis. *Runaway Dream: Born to Run and Bruce Springsteen's American Vision.* Bloomsbury Press, 2009.

Meola, Eric. *Streets of Fire: Bruce Springsteen in Photographs and Lyrics 1977–1979.* It Books/HarperCollins, 2012.

Pelley, Scott. "Springsteen: Silence Is Unpatriotic." *60 Minutes* television interview, October 7, 2007.

Percy, Will. "Rock and Read: Will Percy Interviews Bruce Springsteen," *DoubleTake*, Spring 1998.

Potter-Devening, Carrie. *For Music's Sake: Asbury Park's Upstage Club and Green Mermaid Café: The Untold Stories.* AuthorHouse, 2011.

Remnick, David. "We Are Alive: Bruce Springsteen at Sixty-Two," *The New Yorker*, July 30, 2012.

Rolling Stone Editors. *Bruce Springsteen: The Rolling Stone Files: The Ultimate Compendium of Interviews, Articles, Facts and Opinions from the Files of Rolling Stone.* Hyperion, 1996.

Santelli, Robert. *Greetings from E Street: The Story of Bruce Springsteen and the E Street Band.* Chronicle Books, 2006.

Skinner Sawyers, June, ed. *Racing in the Street: The Bruce Springsteen Reader.* Penguin, 2004.

Springsteen, Bruce. "By the Book," *New York Times*, November 2, 2014.

Springsteen, Bruce. "Letter to the Editor," *Asbury Park Press*, March 31, 2011.

Statham, Craig. *Springsteen: Saint in the City: 1949–1974.* Soundcheck Books, 2013.

Stefanko, Frank. *Days of Hope and Dreams: An Intimate Portrait of Bruce Springsteen,* 2nd ed. Insight Editions, 2011.

Stewart, Jon. "Bruce Springsteen's State of the Union," *Rolling Stone*, March 29, 2012.

Walsh, Baillie. *Springsteen & I.* Black Dog Films/RSA Films, 2013.

Zimny, Thom. *The Promise: The Making of Darkness on the Edge of Town*, 2011.

ABOUT THE AUTHOR

Meredith Ochs is a writer, radio personality, musician, photographer, sailor, and world traveler. She is a talk show host and deejay at Sirius XM and a commentator for NPR's *All Things Considered*. Her work has appeared in *Rolling Stone, Entertainment Weekly, Guitar World,* and numerous other publications. Ochs is a long-time resident of Hoboken, New Jersey, and her favorite Springsteen album is *Darkness on the Edge of Town*.

DEDICATION

To JDK, for putting things in perspective.

ACKNOWLEDGMENTS

Thanks to Dana Youlin for guidance and positivity, Jeremy Tepper for finding me a radio home, Carly Sommerstein for always having my back, Liz Weiswasser for excellent advice, Buster for being great company, Bliss Hammocks for the most comfortable writing chair ever . . . and Lawrence Ochs for everything else.

ORCHES...

SEC ROW SEAT

4 PP 14
MAR. 2, 1977

ADMIT ONE ON ABOVE DATE ONLY

PACE CONCERTS

BRUCE SPRINGSTEEN

AND

THE E STREET BAND

C1.5
17
PRICE
SECTION/AISLE
84

BRUCE SPRINGSTEEN
CIVIC CENTER AUDITORIUM
ATLANTA, GEORGIA
WEDNESDAY
8:00 P.M.

M A R
1 9 7 7

N

ROSEMONT HORIZON
MAR 17 1988 7:30 PM

BRUCE SPRINGSTEEN'S
...EL OF LOVE EXPRESS
FEATURING
E STREET BAND

BRUCE SPRINGSTEEN AND THE E STREET BAND
FESTIVAL EAST PRESENTATION

SEPT 25 1984

BUFFALO
MEM. AUD.
TUE. 8 PM

ADMIT ONE

NO EXCHANGES
PRICE
NO REFUNDS

...BOWL/DALLAS...
HELEY COMMUNITY THTR.
ALSTON WAY
...RESENTS
...EEN

CITY-TV
...SPRINGSTEEN
...OR SHINE
GRANDSTAND
ON JUL 23 1984 8 PM
$.25 CNE USERS FEE
GATE 4
ROW 28
SEC.
NO REFUND • NO EXCH...
WEDNESDAY
PIT
ROW

14
RA
seat 9
row
$19
tax

AT MO...
BILL GRA...
BRUCE S...
WORLD
THU OCT

ALEX COOLEY & 96 ROCK
PRESENT

BRUCE SPRINGSTE...
CIVIC CENTER AUDITO...
ATLANTA...
1 9 7...

BSZ
EVEN
22
SEC
SECTION/AISLE
13
PRICE

BRUCE SPRINGSTEEN

ALEX COOLEY PRESENT

CIVIC CENTER AUDITORIUM

2

BRUCE SPRINGSTEEN

BRUCE SPRINGSTEEN
CHUM, CHUM-FM &
LABATT'S BLUE
GRANDSTAND/RAIN OR S
CNE USERS
24 1984 8 P
ADULT
admission

BSX1
event code
1838 WEST
82 FLOOR
gate/aisle
FL15 ADULT
admission
CAS
R
row
A $ 19.7
price
82
seat CNEA1

PACE CONCERT
presents

Bruce Spri
CONVENTION CE
★ ★ ★ ★
P.M.
9
DEC.

FLOOR SEAT
SEC ROW 19
MAY 30 4, 1976
ADMIT ONE ON ABOVE DATE ONLY

BE-BOP PRODUCTIONS
presents
AN EVENING WITH
BRUCE
SPRINGSTEEN ★
MISSISSIPPI COLISEUM
Jackson, Miss.
TUES. EVE.
8:00 P.M.
4 MAY
1976
NO REFUND PRICE NO EXCHANGE
$6.00

CHUM

BSX2
event code
1943 ENTER
GTE 4
gate/aisle
ADULT
admission
CNEA1
95

MAIN

SEC ROW 30
FLOOR

SECTION/AISLE
SEC 2 13 24 A
ROW/BOX SEAT
NORTH AISLE
22.50
PRICE

ROSEMONT HORIZON
BRUCE SPRINGSTEEN
THU MAR

TOUR
OCT 8 1992

IMAGE CREDITS

ENVELOPE

RIGHT | Bruce Springsteen on the *Born in the U.S.A.* tour, October 1, 1984.

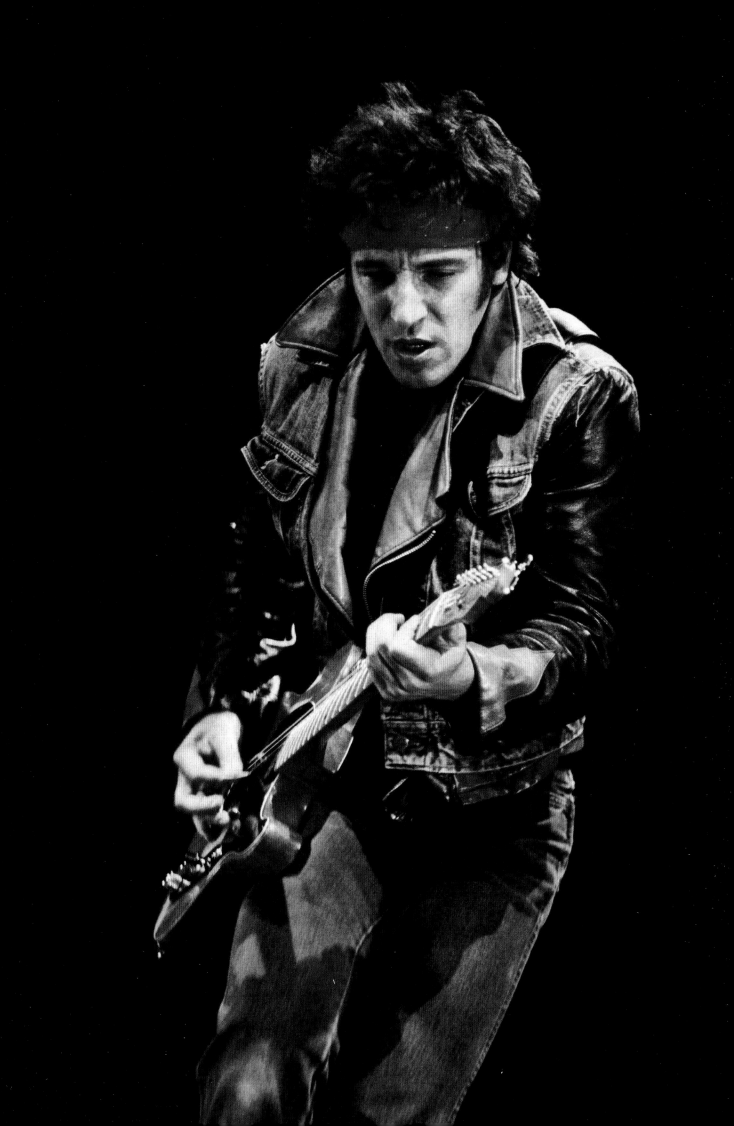

Quarto

© 2023 Quarto Publishing Group USA Inc.

This edition published in 2023 by Chartwell Books,
an imprint of The Quarto Group
142 West 36th Street, 4th Floor
New York, NY 10018 USA
T (212) 779-4972 F (212) 779-6058
www.Quarto.com

First published as *The Bruce Springsteen Vault* in 2015 by Metro Books
an imprint of Sterling Publishing
1166 Avenue of the Americas
New York, NY 10036

10 9 8 7 6 5 4 3 2 1

Chartwell titles are also available at discount for retail, wholesale,
promotional, and bulk purchase. For details, contact the Special Sales
Manager by email at specialsales@quarto.com or by mail at The Quarto
Group, Attn: Special Sales Manager, 100 Cummings Center Suite 265D,
Beverly, MA 01915, USA.

ISBN: 978-0-7858-4375-7

Design: Rosebud Eustace
Editorial: Dana Youlin and Sara Addicott
Image Research: Emily Zach and Donna Metcalf
Production: Tom Miller

Note: All removable documents and memorabilia are reproductions of
original items and are not originals themselves.

Printed in China

PAGE 2 | Bruce performing at the MCI Center in
Washington, DC, on the second night of The Rising
tour, August 10, 2002. The album The Rising was
Springsteen's response to 9/11; the tour ran through
October 4, 2003 and included 120 shows.

PAGE 3 | Bruce and the E Street Band worked a bit of
Wilson Pickett's "Land of 1000 Dances" into his song,
"Light of Day" during this concert at Westfallenhalle in
Dortmund, Germany on April 4, 1993.